"Yes, it is in his own words! I could hear Bob speaking and at one point was waiting for him to offer me some Danish Akvavit! It's a wonderful introduction to those who didn't know Bob Simon, and should, and a cherished souvenir for those who did know him and need their dose of Bob from time to time."

— Gino Francesconi,
Director of Carnegie Hall Archives & Rose Museum

"I didn't know Bob's early life before reading Kristina's captivating interviews but was delighted to see in his cheerful telling of childhood travels in Europe, of teaching himself 'not to be intimidated,' of negotiating (successfully) with banks during the Great Depression, the larger-than-life Bob I knew as a friend and advisor to my nonprofit. Bob was a visionary who never lost faith in big ideas. His heart – and maybe his father's admonition when he was six to 'take care of your mother and sisters' – was the core of his vision of 'community!'"

— Judy Scott Feldman,
Founder and Chair of the National Mall Coalition

"Reading *In His Own Words* is like sitting in a cozy cafe talking with an old friend. In his own buoyant voice Bob Simon tells us vivid stories about his culturally rich Manhattan childhood, his trepidation at becoming President of Carnegie Hall at age 23, and his passion for creating an urban New Town from scratch in the woods and fields of Northern Virginia. For those of us who knew and loved Bob Simon reading these stories is a treat. For those of you who want to learn about this remarkable man *In His Own Words* is a great place to start."

— Vicky Wingert
Former CEO of the Reston Association

In His Own Words

STORIES FROM THE EXTRAORDINARY LIFE OF
RESTON'S FOUNDER, ROBERT E. SIMON JR.

Great Owl Books
GreatOwlBooks.com
Available at:
https://squareup.com/store/great-owl-books

Creative design consultant:
Eric MacDicken

Cover photo:
© Ron Blunt

Candle Light Memorial Vigil:
Courtesy Charlotte Geary Photography

Author photo:
Courtesy of Kristina S. Alcorn

In His Own Words

Stories from the Extraordinary Life of
Reston's Founder, Robert E. Simon Jr.

by Kristina S. Alcorn

GREAT OWL
Great Owl Books

For Walter, Ryan, and Delia.

Acknowledgements

Bob was all about community. So it seems especially fitting that this Bob-centric project engendered its own community – one that grew exponentially as the work progressed. Help came from old friends, people I'd just met, people I'd never met. It came just when I needed it and when I wasn't expecting it at all. This book simply would not exist without the support of this group and while words fail to adequately express my gratitude, here are a few.

First, an enormous thank you to my family for their unfailing support and encouragement. Thank you, Walter and Delia for edits and critiques; Ryan for always believing I could do this; Hillary, Jim, and my mother Carolyn for enthusiasm and marketing savvy (who knew?); and my nephew Kris for conceptualizing the Great Owl Books logo. And to my extended family, my neighbors on Great Owl Circus, who personify the meaning of community.

So many friends selflessly offered their time, talents, and insights. Thank you Rick Golden for reigniting the spark and shepherding me through the process with limitless humor and huevos rancheros; Sara Hartwell and Janie Harris for early reads and infectious optimism; fellow Seahawk Colleen Boyle Stanley and her mother Carolyn Boyle for a treasure trove of early Reston artifacts; Sean Bahrami for saying yes to countless favors; Caroline Schor-MacDicken for generously sharing her considerable talents; and Eric MacDicken for patiently and creatively consulting, and innovating an inspired book design that elegantly presents Bob's life stories.

And then there's the greater community of people who loved Bob and jumped in unconditionally. Thanks to Lynn Lilienthal for boundless enthusiasm and fearless fundraising; Chuck Veatch for a foreword that beautifully encapsulates Bob and Reston; Shelley Mastran and Katie Jones of the Reston

Historic Trust for archival research support; Rebekah Wingert-Jabi and Vicky Wingert for generous sharing of Restoniana; Charlotte Geary for her exquisite photography; Margaret Gupta and Sarah Brittin for copy editing; Tom Langman for sharing early Reston marketing materials; and Gino Francesconi for access to the Carnegie archives and a hand on the back that said, "keep going!"

This book never would have made it off my computer and in to your hands without the financial support of Chuck Veatch, David Ross, and Bill Bouie. Thank you, all.

And most importantly, I owe an enormous debt of gratitude to Cheryl Terio-Simon for trusting me to tell Bob's stories and helping me get them right.

— Kristina

Foreword

I first met Bob Simon in the summer of 1964. I was a newly minted graduate of the University of Virginia and Bob was the 'big boss,' the man from Manhattan, behind the development of Reston. I was hired to help sell the first group of 228 townhouses in the Lake Anne area. At the time no one lived or worked in Reston. Our first business moved to Isaac Newton Square in November 1964. Our first residents moved into Waterview Cluster in December.

Although our sales staff presumptive job was to sell houses, our real job was to sell the concept of Reston. People of all ages, races, and economic status were welcomed to "Live, Work, and Play" in one community. Large natural areas were set aside, permanently, as part of the Master Plan. Recreation, from swimming, golf and tennis, to art galleries and community theatre were under construction or coming soon. The social fabric of the community was being built with the same tenacity as sewer lines, roads, and houses. This emphasis on social fabric was truly the Robert E. Simon in Reston.

There are many of us that made Reston a major part of our lives and livelihood long after Bob was 'deposed' as the leader of this unusual experiment in 1967. But the unique formula for creating community he fashioned was never lost through the ensuing years and succeeding developers. The genius of the Master Development Plan plus the strength of community involvement has stood the test of time. With 62,000 residents and nearly that many jobs, Reston is an example to the world of a terrific place to call home.

Over the years my relationship with Bob changed from employer, to good friend and then with our wives, traveling companions, and ultimately very much like family. We shared anniversaries and birthdays and many, many lunches and dinners. Bob was a great storyteller and as you will read in this wonderful book, he led an amazing life. Kristina Alcorn has not only captured wonderful life stories from Bob, but has framed them with comments, quotes from others and historical references, expanding our understanding of time and place.

Wherever life took him, or in most cases where he took life, Bob sought out people and observed their way of living. It is apparent that these experiences are what informed the creative thinking behind the Reston concept; people and community come first.

All who knew Bob will love these stories and hear his cheerful voice in every tale. For those who did not, you now have the pleasure of getting to know our Founder. Be prepared to meet a fabulous fellow.

Charles A. "Chuck" Veatch
Friend of Bob
Publisher/Creator of the book, *The Nature of Reston*
Simon Fellow – The Best of Reston
Board Member – Reston Historic Trust
Lived, Worked, Played and/or Served in Reston since 1964

Introduction

To those of us growing up in 1970s Reston, Virginia, Robert E. Simon Jr. was an icon. We called him Bob, assuming (correctly) that he'd want us to. Everyone knew of Bob – we waved to him along parade routes and bragged to visitors and newcomers that Bob's initials provided the RES of Reston – but I never met anyone who actually knew him. So fixed was the Founder Legend, I had no idea that he'd been long gone before my family moved to Reston in 1973. I thought he'd always been here, watching over and shepherding his creation. I've found I'm not alone in this misconception.

Decades later, whenever I encountered Bob at local events I leaned in to eavesdrop on anecdotes of his long, fascinating life. I found myself transported to other eras, envisioning the scenes he created – a windowless speakeasy where he first tasted gin, a dusty southwestern rodeo, an opulent ballroom in war-ravaged London where he jitterbugged with British starlets, and a ringside seat in Manila for the fight of the century. And I was awed by his affiliation with some of the most famous artists, politicians, and characters of the 20th century.

His stories begged the question, who is this man? What other adventures had he had? And most importantly to me, how did he become the one who would sculpt a thriving community out of a cow pasture, a whiskey distillery, and a nudist colony? I had to know. So, one evening at a political fundraising dinner, I conceived a plan for a private audience. I asked Bob if anyone had recorded his stories. "Nope," he replied.

A few days later, with a cheap, black tape recorder and notebook in hand, I set off for our first meeting at Bob's apartment. Seconds after I dialed the intercom he answered in a particularly spry voice. He said, as he would at the beginning of each visit, "I'll buzz you in and hope for the best!" Luck was on my side that day and the ambivalent elevator delivered me to the 13th floor. Bob and Boris, his personable cat, welcomed me warmly and led me out to the balcony. We three would spend many afternoons there, high above it all, talking for hours until my tape ran out or muffled sounds from the Plaza below brought us back to the present.

Before recording that first day, Bob and I spoke briefly about just what it was we were doing. I reiterated my desire to preserve and share the stories I'd enjoyed so much. "Okay, fine then. Where do we start?" And so began a long and mutually beneficial collaboration. It allowed Bob to relive old times – predominantly the good ones – and gave me a master class in 20th-century history, culture, the arts, politics, and urban planning – not to mention a cherished friendship with Bob and his wife Cheryl.

I think it's worth mentioning that Bob was 84 when we began our project. His recall was remarkable then and remained so for the better part of his subsequent years. In fact, just a week before his death on September 21, 2015, he corrected me on the proper phrasing of a song he sang with a quartet some eight decades earlier.

As I pulled together the stories for this collection, I came up with questions I wished I'd asked him. Fortunately, I found many of the answers in interviews I recorded years ago with one of his first employees, Jane Wilhelm, and in many other sources still among us – chiefly his wife Cheryl; stepdaughter Lynn Lilienthal; early Reston employee and friend Chuck Veatch; and Carnegie Hall Archivist Gino Francesconi.

I also came across a host of misperceptions of Bob, his motivations, and the nature of Reston. Some believed Bob was the playboy scion of the Simon & Schuster publishing family or an oil baron indulging a fleeting interest in a vanity project. Others believed he was in it solely for profit. The community itself didn't fare much better: critics disparaged Reston as an exclusive country club, a communist enclave, and a hippy commune.

At any rate, in the pages that follow, I present Bob's narrative with minor editing for brevity and organization. In some instances I've added historical background and insights from secondary sources and from former colleagues, friends, and family members to give the reader additional context. Bob knew how to spin a yarn; he charmed even those who could finish the tale for him. In this spirit, I've endeavored to step out of the way and let Bob tell you his stories.

Contents

The Simon Family

Robert E. Jr.   Elsa   Helen

Elizabeth (Betty)   Carol

Edward S. Simon 1835 – 1916	Pauline (Morgenthau) Simon 1848 – 1915	Martin Weil 1839 – 1901	Malvina Weil 1849 – 1931

Robert E. Simon, Sr
1877 – 1935

Elsa (Weil) Simon
1885 – 1964

Elizabeth (Betty) 1910	Helen 1911	Robert E. Jr 1914	Carol 1916

Part 1: The Early Years

Family

Like most people, I had four grandparents. All from Germany, all Jewish, but none religious. My parents were brought up with no religion at all. My maternal grandfather Martin Weil was a piano player. As a young man and a recent immigrant to the United States, he visited the White House. As the family story goes, he turned to the guide and asked if anybody would mind if he tried out the piano. Granted permission, he sat down to play. Soon after he began, a drawn figure with a long beard entered and listened.

When he finished, President Lincoln said, "Young man, your music hath charm."

Robert E. Simon Sr.

My father quit school at 14 to support the family. He got a job as a stock boy in a ribbon factory. He very industriously took the samples and filled the boxes with the corresponding ribbons. He'd been there a couple of weeks and all hell broke loose; it turned out he was colorblind. He left the ribbon factory and got in to a real estate firm called L. J. Phillips as an office boy. In those days, office boys were paid so little that everybody had them. They sat on benches near the door and waited for someone to need coffee, or stamps, or to deliver a package. That's how he started. By 21 he was a partner in the firm.

My father left L. J. Phillips to go into business with my uncle, Henry Morgenthau.[1]

---

[1] Lawyer, businessman, and the most noted American to speak out against the Armenian Genocide as U.S. Ambassador to the Ottoman Empire during World War I.

They stayed busy buying up corners designated to be subway stations before the stations were built. In those days, nobody bought stocks; they bought lots. My father saved up to buy lots in Long Island and other places and then auctioned off the property. On one occasion he got approval from the fire department to light up a house in a spectacular sight. When the flames were going like crazy and people were gathering to see the fire he started the auction. He was a very creative man.

Martin Weil　　　　　　　　　*Robert E. Simon Sr.*

Elsa Weil

My father met Elsa Weil, the only one of her seven siblings to go to college. She was the youngest one of the bunch. My father was a little awe-struck by this glorious beauty on the Vassar Daisy Chain. He courted her, but he wasn't willing to marry her until he could afford to give her a maid, because in those days even maids had maids. He had to be sure he could take care of her sisters and her mother. So he held off

Elsa Weil

popping the question until 1909, when he was 32 and she was 24.

We had a Model T Ford and it was not uncommon for us to go on Sunday drives. On one occasion, we came to a fairly sharp right turn and the steering didn't work. The car turned over and spread us all over the countryside. My father was under the car. This is true – so help me God – my mother raised the damn thing with one hand and pulled my father out with the other.

Bianca Simon

My Aunt Bianca had the misfortune of being born 50 years too early. Today she'd be running IBM. She was a woman ahead of her time, and she took out her frustrations in a creative way on my three sisters and me. Aunt B, as she was affectionately known, put on theatricals. She made the costumes, trained the cast, and directed the shows. When my mother gave birth to her last child, my youngest sister Carol, she came home to another sort of production. Aunt B had recruited several neighborhood kids to put on *Hansel and Gretel* with arias as written by Humperdinck. Though I wasn't quite three, I was cast in the pivotal role of the Dew Fairy. My sisters dressed me in a pink gossamer costume with spangled wings. I learned my arias perfectly and prepared to go on. When it came time for the performance, a group of neighbors gathered to watch. From the wings, I sized up the crowd. Among the familiar

Aunt B (seated) with her parents Edward and Pauline Simon behind her.

faces I saw a stranger in the audience with an enormous black beard. I'd never seen anything like it and decided then and there that my performance was not to be. The show went on without the Dew Fairy.

Bob and sister Betty in costume for an Aunt B theatrical.

Childhood

Bob's mother lovingly chronicled his earliest years. From his baby journal we learn he was born at 12:40 a.m. on April 10, 1914, weighing in at 7 pounds, 7 ounces, and sporting a lush head of hair (a lock of which is preserved in his baby book). She declared him the spitting image of his father. At 4 months he laughed merrily and by 5½ he had an "unusually infectious, hearty laugh and a great sense of humor." He spoke his first word at just

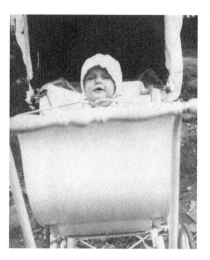

7 pounds, 7 ounces, and sporting a lush head of hair

over a year – "Luha" – which the family understood to mean "thank you." It would be another six months before he mastered "please."

Bob took his first steps at 16 months and "from this day on, Robert made constant progress." He was a natural acrobat[2] and displayed talent for tennis, swimming, and iceskating by the age of 5. He loved to sing and did so in multiple languages; on Christmas Day 1916 he sang English and German carols all day long.

At 4, he began to "pick out lines on the piano":

I started playing the piano when I was 4. At 6, I composed my major composition. To this day, it is my major composition. It was an Indian war dance. Obviously, I was considered to be some kind of a genius, but that was the pinnacle of my career.

On my 6th birthday I was given a scooter. I was damned if I was just going to scoot along at a normal pace. The whole family came out to watch me go down the hill into Riverside Drive.[3] It was so bumpy that I upended and ended up on my nose – I broke it. Happy birthday!

---

[2]   A talent that lasted well into his eighties.
[3]   The family home was at 404 Riverside Drive in Manhattan.

Bob between his sisters Betty and Helen.

Within a few blocks of my neighborhood there was a vegetable store and a meat store. My mother would give me slips to give to Joe, the vegetable man, and Carl, the meat man. I would scoot away from the house with these slips, deliver them to the various merchants, and then scoot up to school on 120th Street. The exciting part was coming home because it was all downhill. The slope was such that I could get up enough speed to pass cars on my scooter. That was absolutely heavenly.

I was pudgy. At one point my sisters demanded that my parents put me on a diet. I went to my Boy Scout master, Bobby Payne, for consolation. He told me to tell them that this was just puppy fat. He was right. I had lines on my door to record height, and I swear I grew 8 inches in one year.

When I was six, my father went to Alaska for a couple of weeks. This is a significant thing in my memory because at that time he said to me, "Now while I'm gone, I want you to take care of your mother and your sisters." That made an impression then and continued to make an impression on everybody.

Bob in his mother's lap between sisters Betty and Helen.

Germany-Austria-Switzerland-France-Belgium-Holland and England

In 1920 my father took a contract to buy the Paramount Building on 44th Street. He sold the contract without ever taking title and made a substantial profit. So now, here is one of my favorite things about my old man. What did he do? Did he say, now I have a quarter of a million dollars and I'll turn it into one or two million? No, he told his office, "I'm leaving you guys for 15 months; I'm taking my family to Europe." That's what he did. We went to Germany-Austria-Switzerland-France-Belgium-Holland and England. We used to say it that way like the Rosary. Some of the highlights were – I got my first suit in London: shorts and a jacket; I got my hair cut in a bob – it was my father's birthday wish.

Bob (in shorts and cap) and family with Tower Bridge in the background.

Crash

There was a real highlight the first summer. We had a Mercedes-Benz with a chauffeur driving with the six of us, my Aunt B who was with us a good part of the time, and 22 pieces of luggage on top. You can imagine what it was like to cross the border: we weren't always welcome. In 1920–21, inflation in Germany was such that my father had to go to the bank every day to get a satchel full of money. Border guards did not always greet us warmly. They made us take every piece of luggage down to be opened and searched. At any rate, once we crossed over from Germany into Austria we were up in the Austrian Tyrolean mountains at a hairpin turn when a convertible, seven-passenger sedan came barreling down. Our driver reacted badly and caused a collision. Several of us were hit by flying glass. I was sitting up front with my father and we both punched our heads through the windshield. My sister was in the back, her throat was cut, her jugular was exposed, and my kid sister was cut, as was I. We lay out on the grass. A stroke of pure luck, two minutes later, a touring car came along with a couple of doctors. They bandaged us up, told us not to move, and they headed down the mountain to the nearest resort town.

The peasants gathered to watch the scene, left when it started to rain, and came back with umbrellas to keep themselves dry. They just watched. My aunt spoke perfect German but they wouldn't respond to her. After all, they were the defated nation, suffering from hideous inflation, and here we were with a chauffeured car. They just sat and gawked at us, offered us nothing, not even water.

The doctors took their time coming back but when they did they brought a truck full of straw and two stretcher-bearers. They didn't expect my sister to still be alive, and finding that she was, they didn't think she could take the ride down the mountain. So they carried her down. They brought us to a resort. It was absolutely full but volunteers surrendered their rooms for us. It was quite touching. We were there for three weeks.

Bob and his family convalescing in an Austrian resort with bandages still visible.

While my sister was recovering, we were equipped with Tyrolean outfits and I played with the kids up and down the hill.

We had attended Christian Science Sunday School. You know, the Christian Scientists say, "The Truth Shall Set You Free." They don't have doctors; you know the truth and that will fix everything up. After we got back from the trip, I found myself giving the following testimonial concerning our ordeal, "We knew the truth and the doctors came." It broke up the whole congregation.

"We were equipped with Tyrolean outfits."

L'Ecole Lafayette

When we got to Switzerland, we had to shift gears. Millie Zelig, a young, Swiss, French-speaking woman stayed with us. We were on a crash program to stop speaking German and start speaking French. That was where we spent the winter before going to Paris. We attended a French school, L'Ecole Lafayette, and the instruction was all in French. In six months we all were fluent. I was seven, my older sisters were nine and eleven, my kid sister was five, but the fluency lasted for the rest of our lives.

I only flunked one course: English. The teacher spoke English with a thick French accent, so I knew she didn't know what she was doing. She got her vocabulary all mixed up. She called an "apron" a "pinafore" and a "bureau" a "chest of drawers." Well, we all knew better than that. We studied like hell at night, we weren't kidding around. I was seven. At that age, you just do it. My little sister cried the first few days.

"Millie Zelig, a young, Swiss, French-speaking woman stayed with us."

Lunch with the Locals

At noon we'd break from school and have lunch with a local family – a mother, father, and two children. We were absolutely astonished at what went on there. The kids got drops of wine in their water. We'd never even had a soda pop. Madame carved bread against her ample bosom. She broke off the bread and mopped up the sauce with her hand. Well, we'd never seen anything like this.

Romeo and Juliet

During this trip we went to the Paris opera house for Wagner. Someone got sick and they canceled *Die Walküre. Romeo and Juliet* was the replacement. So my father and mother huddled to discuss whether or not we should be exposed to this rather racy story, even though it was opera. Finally, it was decided that we could see it. So without any more preparation we sat down to watch *Romeo and Juliet.*

Elementary School

We moved into 404 Riverside Drive with stunning views of the Hudson River to go to the Horace Mann School – the laboratory for the Teacher's College of Columbia University. We didn't understand what was going on at the time; all we knew was there were always people standing behind us taking notes. That's just what school was. The teachers were fabulous. I can tell you every teacher I had:

- 1st grade: Miss Batcheler (we called her Batchy). I stayed in touch with her until she died at 99. Back in those days, if you made it to 100 you got a letter from the president. She made fun of it when she was 95, but as she inched closer she was looking forward to it. She missed by a couple of months.
- 2nd grade: Mrs. Meadowcroft
- 3rd grade: Miss Lewis – a beautiful blond; we were all in love with her.
- 4th grade: I missed; we were in France.
- 5th grade: Miss Condry – a nature lady. We did things like watch cocoons.
- 6th grade: "Rubber Nose" Boyst. It was "Rubber Nose" because of the way she cleared her sinuses. It was a two-finger job: one on each side.

Horace Mann was co-ed. At the end of 6th grade we went up to the boys' school at 246th Street in Riverdale. This was quite different, because it was not connected to a teacher's college. It was not experimental in any way. It was meat and potatoes and wonderful.

The Music Club

In high school we had a group called the Music Club. Fifteen of us would meet in the basement after hours and do whatever we wanted to do. We decided to ask our fellow alumnus, George Gershwin, to come play for us.

It didn't occur to us to let anyone else know about this concert. He was a very good sport and played for our small group. I'm sure he was expecting a larger crowd. I recall he played "Lady Be Good" and toyed with the melody for a long time.

Seymour Durst

One of the guys in our class was a guy by the name of Seymore Durst. His father was in the real estate business – one of the mega-fortunes. His father's advice was, "Don't do anything you can't walk to and never sell anything." He did quite well – he's in the Fortune 500. His son Robert Durst was another story. His brothers had bodyguards to keep them safe from Robert.[4]

Girls

When I was a sophomore in high school or younger, my middle sister had a group of friends. I knew most of them pretty well because they came around the house now and again. One Saturday morning I was minding my own business when one of them, Jane Benedict, called me and said she was having a bridge party with 16 girls, and 1 of the girls had dropped out. She couldn't call a friend at this point because it would be quite an insult. She asked me to fill in, so I did. There were 15 girls and me playing bridge and having lunch. This accounts for some of my lack of terror at running into the female of the species.

Diving

I wanted a varsity letter, but I was very slow, so I knew it wasn't going to happen in track and field. One day I was there at school in my Boy Scout

---

[4] Robert Durst was implicated in three separate murders, which are fictionalized in the 2010 movie *All Good Things* and are the subject of a 2015 HBO series, *The Jinx: The Life and Deaths of Robert Durst*.

uniform and the swim and dive coach said, "Get out of that monkey suit; you're coming with us." So I decided I could earn the letter by learning how to dive. My most heroic high school moment came on the diving team. We had a very good number one and number two on the team; I was number three. So there I was alongside the diving hero – James was his last name – a football player who had hair on his chest while I was struggling to grow pubic hair. Can you believe that my team placed 1st, 2nd, and 3rd? And the football player was 3rd? That was a great moment.

The other great moment occurred during a meet against New York Military Academy. They had a very, very strong team. We regularly limbered up on the board before the meet without suits on. We had suits that were so small and of such fine silk that I could hide the entire suit in my fist. I'd hold out both fists and ask my sisters to guess which hand held the suit. Generally we didn't wear them. So I get out there to do my thing and there was a peal of feminine shrieking; we didn't often have an audience for our meets. These military guys had brought their girlfriends. I turned around, ran quickly down the ladder, and put on my suit.

I had a friend named Stinky Davis; that's what we called him. He was very sophisticated. His parents were not uptight and square;, they were Bohemian. So I spent an overnight with him once and somehow or another we got into apricot brandy. I got in a lot of trouble with the swim coach during practice the next morning. I missed the board while I was warming up. He came over, grabbed me by the head, and smelled my breath. When we had our Monday critique, he really let me have it.

New Technology

When I was about 15, radio was just beginning. My father bought a whole bunch of parts, and he and I put a radio together. This is not my forte, but we got it done. It was a crystal set. You manipulated the wire and crystal to get your station. One day I was sitting there and I got Chicago. I hung on to it for dear life until my father came home. Just as I got him to the radio, they said, "This broadcast has been courtesy of a New York station." At any rate, it was quite exciting to make the radio work. Not long after, my father took me to a fair. He went into one booth and I went into another booth. We could see each other. This was an early form of television, but this was years before television was commercial.

Helen on Bob's shoulders at Blue Mountain Lake.

Summers

My family used to spend summers at Blue Mountain Lake in the Adirondacks. Besides all the tennis and swimming and stuff like that there, I spent a lot of time getting a chipmunk to relate to me, and he finally did. I had more patience then than I've had since. Using food, he eventually came over and would eat out of my hand.

Sundown Ranch

My junior and senior years I went out west to the Sundown Ranch in Arizona. This was a working cattle ranch that took in about 60 dudes. Fred Turley was the owner. His brother had a ranch nearby that took in girls. These were two fabulous summers. The first day, one of the cowhands took us out for a ride and made sure that everyone fell off at least once. He wanted us to learn that falling off wasn't to be dreaded, that we shouldn't be chicken. We were each given a horse that had never been touched, and it was our job to train it and compete with it by the end of the summer. I got a two-year-old called Alexander the Great. He seemed to want to learn everything as quickly as he could. He was fast and we did very well in the competitions at the end of the year.

Bob and Alexander the Great.

We had team-timing roping competitions in a corral. One day we were team-tying. My partner's job was to get the head of the beast and I was to get its hind legs, but the damn beast wouldn't move. Time was ticking, so I spread my noose in front of him and got behind him and pushed him into the noose. At just that moment he raised his tail and instantly I was covered from head to toe. We were so used to horseshit that it was nothing at all. I just rolled around in the dirt until it dried up and fell off, and that's how I went to the dance that night. My girl, no other than the mother of Disney chairman Michael Eisner, didn't seem to mind.

Chicago

I didn't tell you of a most wonderful experience on my way out to the ranch. I had to change trains in Chicago. These were the days when you couldn't take a train nonstop to the West. You had to change trains in Chicago because the tracks had a different gauge. So my godmother had a best friend in Chicago, Claire Heinemann. They had arranged that rather than going straight through, I'd stop off for a couple of days. I was instructed to have breakfast before I got to the house. The only thing is, someone forgot to give me the money to buy breakfast. So I gave the address to the cab driver. When I got there, I said, "No, no, this is not the right address. I'm going to a private house, this is a hotel." Well it turned out it was the right address: it was a mansion on the lake. The first thing I did was hit up the Japanese butler for enough money to pay the cab driver.

A darling lady greeted me warmly and asked me if I had had breakfast. I told her the truth. She clapped her hands twice and another Japanese butler appeared and she said, "Breakfast." Then I went upstairs to this incredible room overlooking Lake Michigan, with French doors and a fruit basket. I went downstairs and sat down at the breakfast table. The custom in my house was we'd eat chicken for dinner on the weekend and chicken livers were served for breakfast on Sunday. We'd watch my father carving the chicken liver to be sure he gave everyone a fair shake, and if it didn't look fair, we'd holler. So that's what I knew about chicken livers. This was a time when you couldn't buy chicken livers. You had to buy the whole chicken. To my amazement, I sat down by myself and they brought me a whole chicken liver. I was astonished that anyone would have chicken livers just kicking around in the icebox.

After breakfast, we went through the house. I wanted to show off my culture, so I admired how wonderfully true to the originals these Renaissance paintings around the house were. Well, they were real.

There were two people, no children, and five cars. Each had a convertible, each had a town car with a chauffeur who rode out in the rain, and they had another car for companionship. This really knocked me out. I'd never seen wealth like that before or since.

Snowflake Ranch

My second summer in Arizona, we went to a rodeo at Snowflake Ranch. It was named after the two founders, Mr. Snow and Mr. Flake. Flake was "Granddad Flake" to us. That year we went to Granddad Flake's Mormon funeral. This was back in the day of multiple wives, no alcohol, no coffee, no cigarettes.

A taunting voice over the loudspeaker sought a volunteer steer rider. Outwardly confident, Bob climbed into the chute and sized up the situation:

What I quickly realized is all the dudes who'd gone before could've ridden forever if they ignored the rules – only one hand may grip the steer, the other hand must hold the hat overhead, both legs must ceaselessly rake the sides of the steer so there is no gripping. Of course, I held on with two hands and dug my spurs in tight.

The toughest words in the English language are "Let 'er go." The chute opened and off we went. The horn sounded off the eight seconds, so I assumed I could dismount – no one had thought to discuss that part with me. I hopped off, landed on my back, and felt a burning sensation in a place you don't want to feel a burning sensation. From the ground I looked up and saw that the steer had busted his leg. I hobbled to the chutes where my gang was cheering. A fellow from the local paper asked what happened. I said, "Well, the steer stepped on my nuts and broke his leg!" And that was printed in the Holbrook Gazette.[5]

Christian Science Camp

"Reflections on Perfection is Our Aim" was the theme the first year. This was not a modest proposal. We lived in tents with floorboards on Long Lake near Bridgton, Maine. We'd run up to the soda fountain in town and have ourselves a treat and put some more in our pockets – until one day Mr. Stanley, the head of camp, came to Bridgton too. There he saw all of his campers sitting at the counter having banana splits. That was the last time.

One year we had a couple of counselors from Principia, the Christian Science college. They wore boots and riding britches: these were tough guys. They eventually got thrown out. Among other things they did was a lot of paddling. "Assume the position" – I think that's what they said. That meant, grab your ankles and then they'd belt you with this paddle. It was sadistic.

---

[5]   I failed to find a copy of this article, so we'll just have to take Bob's word for it.

My second year, there was a girls' camp and we had an annual co-ed softball game. We decided we'd catch a skunk. We threw out our ponchos to trap one, and on the day of the big game, we released him behind home plate and he waddled onto the field. After that we were confined to quarters for a while. He sprayed us, but we had our ponchos on. I may be one of the few people who like that smell.

Carnegie Hall

In the early 1920s word got around that Carnegie Hall would be demolished to make way for another concert hall. So my father got a bunch of his friends together. He wanted to get a hold of key corners: together they bought property on 56th and 57th Streets on either side of Carnegie Hall. When Andrew Carnegie died in '25 my father met with Mrs. Carnegie to buy the Hall itself to make a complete acre plot.

At news of the sale, the papers foretold of Carnegie's demise (as they would again in 1960). The opposition predicted a huge commercial structure would erase this legacy of the Age of Innocence. But rather than tear it down and consolidate the acre, Bob's father made an agreement with Mrs. Carnegie to continue theatrical operations for at least five years as long as the Hall turned a profit. Several of his father's innovations, including adding revenue-earning storefronts to the property, ensured the Hall's longevity. The promised five years stretched to decades and as a result, the Simons had first chair boxes for every event.

My mother was conscientious: she'd been brought up not to leave anything on her plate. This applied to the Hall as well. She thought it was our responsibility to fill the box for every damn thing that took place there. I remember having stage seats

for Rachmaninoff. Of course, I heard Kreisler and Heifetz and Duke Ellington and Benny Goodman, and so many others from Box 23. Many evenings my sisters and I huddled in our pajamas saying farewell to these glamorous people, [Bob's parents] going out in evening dress and black tie. Carnegie Hall was very much a part of our lives.

Prohibition

Bob's father strictly adhered to the letter and spirit of the 18th Amendment,[6] going so far as to throw out all the alcohol in the house. Bob was less compliant. As a 15-year-old bass in a quartet rounded out by Mayo, Fox, and Reed (tenor, baritone, and second tenor respectively), Bob didn't protest when the older boys suggested ducking out of school early and taking a detour on their way to a performance at the Horace Mann Girls School.

In those days of prohibition, it wasn't difficult to find a speakeasy. All you had to do was find a storefront with the windows and doors painted black. The police didn't seem to know, but these boys did. They were very sophisticated. So we walked into a speakeasy four blocks from the school. I sat down and waited to see how one should behave; I'd never been in one before. Reed

---

[6] From 1920 to 1933 the production, transport, and sale of alcohol was illegal.

said confidently, "I'll have a Tom Collins." I repeated, "The same." Well, it didn't hurt at all. I mean it was just lovely. Then one of the guys said, "I'll have another," and I mimicked this too. And another! I didn't feel a thing until I got off the stool. So with one guy on either side of me, my arms over their shoulders, we walked up to the school. We took our place on stage before all these girls who had been in my class and now, for God's sake, they were women! And, oh! They were tall and I was so short!

The quartet finished their set with "You Call That Religion?," a popular spiritual of the day. Emboldened by the gin, Bob abandoned the stiff arrangement and carried the song back to its African American roots:

I got into the spirit of the thing, which was NOT part of the act at all. When the boys sang, "You call that religion?" and I sang "No, No!" in a very deep voice – I mean deep – that was my big moment. The alcohol made that big moment so big it was almost frightening, it was so wonderful!

After prohibition, the atmosphere in the Simon household liberalized. During visits home from college, Bob's mother would sneak a sip from his cocktail and say, "Pooh, I don't know how you can drink that stuff!" and then on second thought she'd say, "Make me one."

Marmolada Glacier in Italy

Summer in Europe

In 1929 we decided as a family we should go flying. We took a commercial airline and that was quite an experience. The plane was mighty small. We went over to Europe and back on the German Hamburg–American Alliance. It was incredible: five meals a day – breakfast, bouillon and crackers, lunch, tea, and dinner. At dinner, as a regular phenomenon, there would be two teaspoons of Beluga caviar.

"The plane was mighty small."

Marmolada Glacier

My father, sister, and I, with a couple of guides, went up the Marmolada Glacier in Italy. This was a fairly exciting happening. We came to a place where the lead guide carved a step in a cone to cross the crevasse. One guide pulled my sister across, and there was another one to pull my father across. I was between guides. I stepped, slipped and grabbed the cone. To be helpful, my sister took my walking stick and threw it down the crevasse. In the end, they hoisted me out of there. It was very exciting.

Harvard

ROBERT EDWARD SIMON, Jr.
Born on April 10, 1914, at New York, New York. Prepared at Horace Mann School. Home address: 404 Riverside Drive, New York, New York. In college four years as undergraduate. Kirkland House. Freshman Soccer Squad; House Football Team 1934-35; House Swimming 1932-33; House Squash 1933-34; Glee Club 1931-34; University Choir 1933-35; Junior Usher.

Field of Concentration: History and Literature   Intended Vocation: Business

I was 17. I got on the train, without my family, and headed to Cambridge. It wasn't very hard to get accepted in those days. Anyone who was warm and knew how to read and write could get in. It was the Depression, 1931. I had a ground floor single suite on Harvard Yard with two rooms all to myself.

Harvard's president was Abbott Lawrence Lowell. He was a combination of lineage from the three great Massachusetts families. He had a little dog, a spaniel, which ran ahead of the president, warning those who saw him to straighten up and fly right. In those days we all wore jackets, grey slacks, and saddleback shoes: that was the uniform.

There were professors and people called section men: instructors who met in small groups, gave out assignments, and graded papers. I had been a good high school student, so I wasn't surprised to be a good college student. I was transferred to [a new section man] Paul Cram. I did everything I could to prevent this; I heard he was a real horror. We wrote a paper every week in the section. I read all the history stuff so I could knock him dead on first acquaintance. At the end of that period he handed out the graded blue books. I just about dropped my teeth because instead of A+++, I got a D. It was a real shocker. In those days men didn't cry, period. But I'll confess there were a few little tears in my eyes but I did not cry. Today, I would be sobbing. The last guy left the classroom and I stood there paralyzed. He explained I got the facts perfectly but I hadn't assimilated them. I hadn't made them my own. I had no point of view. Memorizing facts was not what he was about. This was a critical point in my education. Working with him and moving my grade up was quite a revelation.

Sometime in Summertime

My freshman year at Harvard, I rented a piano. I collaborated with Wenner Laise. We had a lot of fun. He was kind of a composer; I was kind of a lyricist. We got one of our compositions played on the local radio station. They promised to play it again a week later. We got lots of our friends to write in to express how much they had enjoyed it on the day they were supposed to play it again. But something happened, they changed the schedule, and it wasn't played again. So our letters all arrived about a piece that hadn't been on the air. Our reputation suffered a little. Walter Donaldson, who was a medium-well-known composer, stole our whole song: lock, stock and barrel. We didn't have a copyright. He took it. I don't remember what we called our song but he called his version "Sometime in Summertime." That was our song. I don't remember it too well, but it was a memorable song!

Kirkland House

One of the things President Lowell had done was produce the house plan. Both Harvard and Yale were modeled after the University system at Oxford and Cambridge. The house would typically have 200–300 occupants. Each house had a common room, a dining room, interior gardens, and a housemaster who lived on the premises. There were house teams: I played on the football team; I was no star, that's for sure. It gave people with no ability a chance to play on teams.

Our housemaster, Edward Whitney, was a mighty handsome fellow, and his wife Peggy was a wonderful lady. They'd invite us to tea. I wasn't used to that. I remember the awful challenge of having a cup of tea in my hand and sitting down and not spilling it all over me.

At Kirkland House we had a "High Table" – a formal dinner – fashioned after the English colleges. At Christmastime we had a banquet. We wore

KIRKLAND HOUSE

tuxedos. It began with a parade of the chefs with the white hats, stuffed goose, suckling pig, and a boar's head – the works.

We also had an event called the "Coffee Pot." Each week we invited a distinguished guest (as distinguished as possible) to join us. We'd eat dinner with the distinguished guest and retire to the lounge where he would do his thing. My senior year I became head of the Coffee Pot. Two of the people I had over are known the world over. Felix Frankfurter, Supreme Court Justice was one. He was a professor at Harvard. He said, "I can answer any question you can ask me." I made sure they asked questions in his field.

Dance with a Pillow

When [my roommate] **Joseph Alban Weber** came to us from Chicago, he was as green as grass. It seems like a contradiction in terms. He was an Eagle Scout. I taught him to dance with a pillow. We had a few sessions on how to make out. I went on the theory that you presented the girl in question with the physical opportunity. If she took the opportunity, then you gave her another opportunity. And you kept on offering opportunities and this way you never got slapped in the face. And you never got turned down. It worked.

Prohibition (Part 2)

It was still Prohibition, so I bought a five-gallon keg of grape juice with instructions on how to turn it into wine. The plan was that the folks who sold it to me would come back and get it after fermentation and bottle it. Well, they didn't come back because they got arrested. So there I was with five gallons in a barrel, and what to do? So I got a hose and some bottles, never realizing that in the process I'd ingest some alcohol along the way. By the time I got to the bottom of the barrel I was really plastered. The wine couldn't have been any good, but I don't remember it at all. I learned that Prohibition was only good for bootleggers and policemen.

Shanty Shane

My sophomore and junior summers I was a counselor at Shanty Shane on Lake Fairlee, Vermont. Between 7:00 and 9:00 a.m., I had all the kids in the place. They ranged in ages from 5 to 13. I had to figure out what to do with this enormous age range of kids. What worked for everyone was Homer: *The Iliad* and *The Odyssey*. I'm not saying they were all sitting up, eyes blazing, but it kept them out of trouble. If I had a particularly grateful parent, rather

Counselor Bob at Shanty Shane on Lake Fairlee (with a happy camper on his shoulders)

than a tip they'd take me over to the Hannover Dartmouth golf course for the day. It was very hazardous with gulches and hills. I loved golf but I gave it up when I was 25; it took up too much time. I couldn't play tennis and golf. There is no comparison: tennis wins out.

At Shanty Shane the counselors shared a cabin. When we wanted a drink, we'd drive down a dirt road and stop at a house. We'd knock on a door and an old lady would put her head out the door and say, "What'll ya have?" We'd say, "Peach or apple or cherry." They'd take alcohol and add some syrup and shake it. That was it. Better with liquor! If memory serves it was Dorothy Parker who said, "Candy is dandy, but liquor is quicker."

Chessie

My junior year I bought a 1931 Chevy convertible for $300. We called that car "Chessie" – damned if I know why. It was a wonderful car. The first time we used it I was in a tux with my girl in the front, Griff and his girl in the back with the rumble seat. We got a flat tire; it happened all the time. So I had to change the tire, lying on the icy road. Griff got his girl and my girl and snuggled in front. There was no heat in the car: no one had thought of that yet. People had to use blankets and lap robes to stay warm.

The Dicks

In Boston there are two main avenues: Commonwealth and Massachusetts. They cross at one point. One winter the snow was six feet or more – so high that you couldn't see around the corner until you got there. So I was going like hell when I came into that intersection and a taxi was doing the same.

"We called that car 'Chessie' - damned if I know why."

There was a great crash. No one was killed. I drove Chessie home and that was that.

That afternoon I'd invited Martyn Green [English actor and singer best known for Gilbert & Sullivan comic operas] and his wife over to lunch at the house. Here we were in the middle of our meal when my roommate Griff came down and told me in melodramatic terms, "The Dicks are out here!" – meaning the police [detectives]. I replied waving my hand in a lofty gesture, "Tell them I'm entertaining and I cannot see them now."

They went away, but soon after I got an invitation to go to the station house where they clapped me into the jug. They took my belt, tie, and fountain pen to be sure I didn't do myself in. So here I was with a bunch of kids. There were six cells on each side. There were no matches allowed, so there was one cigarette going all the time. When it was about to go out, it was passed through the bars to the next guy.

I called my friend Dick Ernst and asked him to quietly go through the dining hall to raise the bail. I told him not to let Whitney, the housemaster, know. I was finding it very interesting listening to these young kids, my cellmates, talking. It seemed to me they were trying to learn to be tough like the guys in the movies, but they were using this language that was not quite their own yet. Four or five hours later they came to make bail for me – my friends and the housemaster. They broke up laughing seeing me with my pants hanging down and without a tie. Those were the days when you didn't see people without ties very often.

So then came the trial. The occupants of the taxi – a woman and her daughter, a ballerina – sued me. I got my sister Betty to get her lawyer friend to defend me. The story was picked up by somebody and got back to my father. He called me on the telephone. He didn't tell me what to do. I told him I had a lawyer and that was it.

The trial was fabulous. I had read Lincoln Steffens's autobiography. As a reporter he'd covered the Tammany Hall trial. He came to the conclusion that probably the crooked government was better for the people than the reformed one. The crooked one got things done. At any rate, his story of that trial came to my rescue on this occasion. The ballerina told the sad story of the accident and how her dancing career was over. She wore dark sunglasses – in those days that wasn't common. I had my lawyer do just what the Lincoln Steffens lawyer had done. He said he'd appreciate it if the ballerina could repeat the highlights for him. She repeated the whole thing: clearly it had been memorized. If you think about it, it has nothing to do with whether it was true or not. But it worked. Outside the courtroom the ballerina took her glasses off and told her mother they had lost. She said she didn't want to play games anymore.

And then came the bill from the lawyer. I told my sister, "That is some fine friend of yours!" You have to understand my mindset. I was getting $50 a month and the bill was $100. I was so inexperienced that I didn't understand how charitable his fee was.

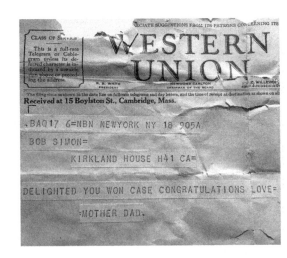

Harvard Glee

I joined the Harvard Glee Club.
We sang Bach's B Minor Mass and
Brahms' Requiem. Our conductor
my first three years was Doc David-
son. He was the first to bring good
music to college glee clubs. Before
then it had been folk songs, college
songs. He was a short little fellow.
He'd get us relaxed, get us laughing. "Not a dry seat in the house,"
he used to say.

In my junior and senior years I sang in the choir. The choir was very
much in demand, so I was damn lucky to get in it. It paid. We sang every
morning during the 15-minute service. On Sundays we were joined by others; Radcliffe joined us sometimes. They paid enough at funerals, so that
when we saw Professor So-and-So had died it was time for celebration. It was
a bloody fortune, $20 – that would be $100 today. With the funerals, the
entire tuition was paid. Tuition for the year was $400; the room with private
bath and living room, $180 a year.

Anti-Semitism

Growing up Jewish was quite a different thing than it is now. My family –
mother, father, grandparents, and cousins – none of our family was religious.
We didn't go to synagogue, didn't do the bar mitzvah, bat mitzvah, etc. We
were sent to Christian Science Sunday school because my Aunt B got involved. I had experienced a little anti-Semitism at Horace Mann School. The
most overt example was the Boy Scout patrol I wanted to join didn't have
any Jews in it, so I didn't get into that one; I got into another one.

At Harvard, the first time I knew anything was going on was when a bunch of guys started to run around the yard. I found out they were pledges for Hasty Pudding. They put on a big show at the end of the year but I never saw one. It was not open to nonmembers. Hasty Pudding was the doorway to the final clubs [exclusive, secretive, all-male clubs]. It was open to everyone who was WASPily acceptable. They had no Jews in Hasty Pudding, so they had no Jews in the final clubs. Of all the finals, the Porcellian was the toughest club to get into. You had to be very rich and very well born and have lineage back to the Mayflower if not back to Pocahontas. There were other clubs that didn't require as much. There were a couple of fraternities; there was a Jewish fraternity. I didn't want to be part of that. There is no question that I went through Harvard as a second-class citizen. There was this whole world of society that was not open to Jews.

In New York you could read a list of the patrons of the board of directors of the Metropolitan Museum, the Metropolitan Opera, the Philharmonic and you wouldn't find a Jewish name on any of them. Today it's quite a different story. Believe it or not, getting into the Harvard Club of New York wasn't an easy thing, and I got in. One would think that anyone who had gone to Harvard would be admitted, but that was not the case.

The Fruiter

In June 1935, after graduation, I had plans to go to Europe with my friend Dick Ernst. The week before our departure his father turned deathly ill. I was in a quandary as to whether to go alone or not at all. It was not a very pleasant prospect as far as I was concerned. But I found out that that's the very best way to travel. So I booked an American "fruiter," a cargo ship that took 10 days to cross. My room had a single bed and a double bunk. I'm not sure how, but I figured I should have the single bed. There was a nightgown on the single bed and I thought, "Well, maybe on the fruiter they gave you a nightgown." I never had a nightgown on before, so I put it on. The second roommate showed up and I got into bed with the nightgown on. The third roommate got into the top bunk in his underwear. Of course we figured this out before we had been out to sea very long. The third roommate was so portly that his wife had to tie his shoelaces for him: he couldn't reach them. So you can imagine how big that nightgown was.

One of my roommates was a Dane. It turned out he was a count. He was a good guy. We went up to have dinner together and then we went to the saloon. This was a relatively small room; there were only 60 passengers. It had an upright piano and crank phonograph. In no time flat, the Danish count had a girl dancing with him. I didn't think too much of her. I was there in all of my distinguished glory as a Harvard graduate. So, I was picking records and she came up behind me. Every time I picked up a record, she'd say, "That's cute." I couldn't put up with this so I went to bed.

The next morning I walked around to work up an appetite for breakfast. I heard music coming from the saloon and someone was playing the Myra Hess arrangement of "Jesu, Joy of Man's Desiring." This person was bringing out the inner voices, which is not the easiest thing to do. So I hightailed it for this room and my jaw fell through the floor. Who should be playing this piece on the piano but that dumb girl from the night before. Well, it turned out that she was heading to England to study with a distinguished piano coach before playing two concerti with the Minneapolis Symphony Orchestra. Her name was Ramona Gerhard. She was the pianist-on-call at [Minneapolis radio station] WCCO, therefore she could play classical, Victoriana, jazz. So she was a fabulous addition and she played generously for us all the way over.

One of the high points of the trip was playing a ring toss game. You threw a ring over the net. I was in the finals with an Irish priest and the boat was heaving like crazy. One minute you were charging the net, the next you were bouncing off the side of the boat. It was a wonderful trip across.

Bike Trip

I bought a bike and set forth from Edinburgh. The entire two-month period I rode my bike from the Lochs of Scotland all the way down to Land's End/Cornwall – 2,000 miles in all. I had rain one-half day the entire time. Now in 1935, I was a very rare bird as far as the villages where I went "bed-and-breakfasting." Some people had never seen an American. In one or two cases they'd call out the neighbors for a party. I was on a 10- shilling-a-day budget. Breakfasts were very ample. The only thing that took some time

to get used to was the bacon. It was lard swimming in grease, but it was high-energy stuff.

I was not out to prove how fast I could go at all. I wanted to enjoy everything along the way. I had a touring bike with three gears; I sat up and saw the scenery. I was in no hurry. I averaged 50 miles a day. I'd drop in on anything along the way that interested me. It was just wonderful. When I got to Loch Ness I ran into quite a few people who knew somebody who had seen the monster. Nobody had seen it themselves. But the closest I came to it was a bunch of monks in a monastery who were completely convinced they'd seen the monster.

One of my best experiences was climbing up Ben Nevis [the highest mountain in the United Kingdom]. I had to carry my bike on my hip all the way up an unpaved road on the south side. When I got up about halfway, there on the side of the road was one of those idyllic pictures of a family with a blanket spread out, sandwiches being pulled out of the basket, and a thermos for drinks. There was no traffic on this unpaved road. I cast sheep's eyes at this group as they avoided my gaze. So, I struggled on up. When I got to the top, it was past lunchtime so I let it go down the paved northside. I went down faster than the cars.

I hopped a train for Devon and Land's End. Before I got to Devon, I went to a musical camp I had read about. I wrote to them and won a position. The closest analogy I can think of is the Berkshires. They had a full orchestra and chorus and singers. The orchestra was composed of some of the best musicians from all over Britain. They had some stunning singers. Believe it or not, the orchestra, without the chorus, did the first act of the *Die Walküre*. We did choral works.

On the weekends people came from far and near, parked in fields, and nearby bed-and-breakfasts. We put on three concerts as I remember it. Afternoons we'd go off in groups and do madrigals and go hiking and swimming. In the evening, after meals, we would settle down in a large barn with a lovely member of the opposite sex, get a blanket, and there would be a concert, chamber music. It was a wonderful couple of weeks.

When I started biking the first few days, my tail got sore and my legs wished I would quit. But now, I did 120 miles; it was nothing. I was pleased to be in such great condition. I rode from Exeter to London, about 120 miles. I had gone all over, leaving my bike and pack wherever. When I got to the London bed-and-breakfast this time, I though I better take my pack in with me. So I did. But they stole my bell and my luggage carrier. So that was the wicked city compared to the innocent countryside.

"I had a touring bike with three gears; I sat up and saw the scenery. I was in no hurry."

I went over to Paris and got together with the Dammanns.[7] The second day I was there, my cousin Lucille came to my hotel to tell me my father had died: he was 58 years old. The day before, he had been to a doctor because he did not feel well. The doctor gave him a thorough examination and said he was fine. He went home to bed and died the next morning. I booked passage home on an ocean liner. When I came home, my mother and my three sisters were on the dock waiting for me. I'd heard repeated over the years the admonition from my father, to "take care of your mother and sisters," so it seemed quite natural for me to come home and take care of them. They thought so too.

---

[7] Distant relatives.

Part 2: Carnegie Hall and World War II

Corruption at Carnegie Hall

Upon his return to the States, Bob assumed his father's role in the family real estate business and at Carnegie Hall, Inc. He immersed himself in the operations and management aspects of the Hall to a greater extent than his father had. At first, Bob found comfort in the familiar faces of his father's longtime staff.

I'd known everyone in my father's office since childhood. The secretary, Ms. Veit, dandled me on her knee as a little fellow, and Arthur Govern introduced me to the supply closet. I was awestruck by the number of pencils. He let me play with the checkwriting machinery. The head of the office was Murray Weisman. My father had a wonderful office; this was a relatively small operation – 8 people on the 21st floor of 654 Madison Ave. We had one side and Leland Hayward[8] had the other. My father's office had four exposures and a balcony with furniture. I decided I'd keep that office.

But soon Bob began to discover irregularities and a conspiracy of silence. Murray Weisman instructed the staff to hamper Bob's attempts to understand Carnegie Hall operations. Further investigation revealed corruption perpetrated by the men Bob had considered uncles:

---

[8]   Iconic Broadway producer and Hollywood agent.

In 1936 a decision had been made to put in an electric generator in Carnegie Hall. I asked for the rationale for this thing. I was given piles of reports to read. I took them home and I couldn't get the right answer. The figures that I had been given were not working out. I tried to reconstruct it but I just couldn't get it. I came into the office the next day and laid out my concerns. At this point I ceased being the apprentice. I knew that Murray Weisman wasn't what he was supposed to be.

John Weil[9] told me if I wanted to get this thing in focus I should turn up in the engine room that evening. So, that night after a performance, I appeared in a tuxedo. When I arrived I heard some scuttling about – the kind one associates with mice disappearing into their holes. There was our chief engineer and Joseph Lipkoff[10] hoisting an enormous pipe. I played it cool and said something like, "Hi fellas, looks like a pretty big job for just the two of you." The jig was up and they knew it; from the holes in the walls emerged our sheepish Carnegie crew. It turned out our staff had been doing the job, but we were paying Lipkoff as if his staff was doing the work. So this was the denouement. We went down to 40 Wall Street for a meeting with the board of directors. We had a very distinguished board consisting of prominent judges Joseph M. Proskauer, Abraham Elkus, and lawyers Henry Ingraham, Milton Bergerman, and James Rosenberg. This was a high-powered bunch of guys. Murray Weisman made his pitch and I made mine. They fired him and they made me president of Carnegie Hall at 23. I was scared to death.

We also fired the chief engineer and brought in a new one. I asked him to send me statements from the physical plant so I could check how things were working. I realized something was amiss. The ratio of labor to materials was skewed. I found bills for 25 tons of ice for a 20-ton chamber. So I said, "Chief" – he didn't like to be called Chief, but that's what we called him – "Chief, how come?" No answer. So I offered, "Be my guest, I'll buy 25 tons of ice and we'll see how you get it in there." They fit it in there all right, but

---

[9] Bob's cousin and Carnegie Hall employee.
[10] The contractor awarded the job.

they did so with ice picks. That was not the way it was done. That was the end of Chief. Later, I found out that during the war, he had been a contractor all over New York using our personnel and materials without reimbursing Carnegie Hall.

Paying the Rent

It was 1935; it took a while for the depression to sink its teeth in. We had all kinds of properties and couldn't pay the mortgages; no one was paying rent. I went to negotiate our mortgages with the president of the Harlem Savings Bank. I sat down at the great man's desk. I put everything that I needed on a single sheet of paper and got it. I used a trick that I had taught myself to not be intimidated. I imagined him as an old man on his back with his grandchild on his chest with his wife saying, "Get up off the floor you old fool."

The Russian Tea Room

Not long after my father bought Carnegie Hall, Alexander "Sasha" Maeef came to see my father: he wanted to open up a tearoom. My father learned his story. He was a Russian, married with a pregnant wife. Being a white Russian, they grabbed him and put him on the border with China. He was ready to be shot, but the Red Cross came to the camp one day and spirited him across the border into China. He managed to make his way to the US. In Chicago he became a very good headwaiter. He was so good some people said they'd back him if he came to New York. So my father rented him a store at 150 West 57th Street, which was part of the commercial property he had before Carnegie Hall. It was a nice little tearoom. One day a guy came in and looked at the menu. It was tea and crumpets. He looked over and saw that the "helps," as Sasha called them, were enjoying a bowl of borscht.[11] So

---

Years later Bob overheard strangers talking about the best borscht they'd ever had, not in Russia but at Sasha's.

he said, "I'd like a bowl of that." This created a bit of stir, but they came up with some and found a way to price it. And the rest is history. The Russian Tea Room grew and grew.

My relationship with Sasha began soon after I took over for my father in 1935. I built a retail store in Jackson Heights, a suburb of Manhattan. I put Sasha in there. He opened a restaurant and did very well. Then the Club Richman on 56th Street became available. The Club Richman was run by Harry Richman[12] and Lou Schwartz. The second floor had a couple bedrooms and a bathroom. These guys lived up there. Sometime along the way, one of them met a girl by the name of Lucille LeSueur. They installed her up there and shared her amicably until she got to be a bit of a pain in the neck. One day they were entertaining a Hollywood friend of theirs and he was bemoaning the fact that he had four nights on the damn train going out to California and needed a blanket to keep warm. So Harry looked at Lou, Lou looked at Harry, and they said, "We've got just the thing for you." So Lucille got on the train with that guy and it wasn't too long before she changed her name to Joan Crawford.

Toscanini

In 1937 Arturo Toscanini[13] went over to the NBC symphony. When they built Rockefeller Center, they built him Studio 8H.[14] That was an unusual phenomenon in that they insulated that studio from all the steel in the building. It was like a baby in a mother's womb. It was supposed to be perfect acoustics, but nevertheless and notwithstanding, Toscanini chose to move the whole orchestra all the way over to Carnegie Hall at great expense to the management when he was recording. He preferred the acoustics of Carnegie Hall.

---

[12] Singer, actor, dancer, and nightclub performer whose career was cut short by an overpowering personality and limited acting skills.
[13] World-renowned Italian virtuoso conductor.
[14] Since converted into a television studio that now houses *Saturday Night Live*.

Carnegie Hall at 50

In 1941 we celebrated the 50th anniversary of Carnegie Hall. So many artists returned to perform: Toscanini, Heifetz, Rachmaninoff, Horowitz, Marian Anderson, Paul Robeson – many others. That same year I got a $15,000 grant from the Carnegie Foundation (today it would be $100,000) for a lecture series and book on the theme, "Be Your Own Music Critic." The idea was to liberate people from the necessity of reading the criticisms the next day to see how they had enjoyed it. So we had a whole bunch of very distinguished people participate. Olin Downs was the critic at the time for the *New York Times*; there was no other critic of his standing. He was to be the master of ceremonies. The first lecture was very traumatic for me because Olin Downs didn't show up. I had to take over and I'd had no public speaking experience worth mentioning.

Summer Opera

We managed to get some people interested in light opera in the summer. There were several problems connected with that, primarily that we had no air conditioning. This was solved by our chief engineer who took two coils from an antiquated system, turned them upside down, and ran chilled water through them. We put 20 tons of ice in a chamber off 56th Street and rained water on the ice. The ice water ran through the coils and we blew our air over it. It's not exactly air conditioning, but it worked.

Once we had the air conditioning, we wanted to serve spirited beverages. I sent a telegram to Governor Thomas E. Dewey saying that we needed a liquor license. By God, he said, "Go ahead, folks." It was not allowed in any theater in the city: we were the first public assembly in NYC to have a liquor license.

Caesar Petrillo

In 1942, James Caesar Petrillo, the controversial president of the American Federation of Musicians, called a strike banning musicians from the nation's recording studios until they were paid a royalty on every record sold. President Roosevelt considered music important to national morale during wartime, and Petrillo's actions borderline treasonous. Roosevelt himself asked Petrillo to relent, and the War Production Board ordered him to end the strike. Petrillo refused.

As the most notorious and feared labor union leader of his time, references to Petrillo often appeared in 1940s and 1950s popular culture. A Time magazine cover story renamed him Jimmy "Mussolini" Petrillo. Dinah Washington immortalized him in the song, "Record Ban Blues." She sings,

Talked to a lyric writer.
He was trying to put a song across.
He asked when I'd record again.
I said, "Petrillo's the boss."

Bing Crosby's character defers to Petrillo in the movie, The Bells of St. Mary's, and in the animated short "Hurdy-Gurdy Hare," Bugs Bunny fears reprisal for employing a nonunion, monkey organ-grinder. He quips, "I sure hope Petrillo doesn't hear about this!"

Petrillo also wielded immense power in New York City: he could put a venue, including, of course, Carnegie Hall, on the union's "unfair" list and prevent union members from playing there.

That summer, '42, we were all set to do operetta. Just as we were getting ready to go, we got word from Caesar Petrillo that he wasn't going to let us do it unless we canceled our contract with the Boston Symphony Orchestra. The Boston Symphony was a nonunion orchestra because the philanthropist who had willed them a considerable amount of capital specified that they must stay nonunion. This made it difficult for them to organize, so Petrillo wanted to use the Carnegie Hall contract as a lever to make them join the union. Petrillo was a very short man who single-handedly got the musicians a living wage. But the people who weren't too favorable towards unions in general thought he was a gangster.

So, I started a summer of negotiations with Petrillo, which turned out to be one of the most fun experiences I ever had. He had an office on the East Side. He had a couple of his goons in the lobby casing the joint to be sure the people who went up were okay. They had walkie-talkies, so they could block off the whole floor where he had the office if they had to. So this was quite a business of sitting down with him. He only gave us dispensation for a week at a time, so I met with him weekly the whole summer.

He showed me the pistol he had in his drawer and the autographed photograph of Eleanor Roosevelt on the wall. He let us go all summer and we had a complete season. At the end of the summer, in my last meeting with him, he gave me the greatest compliment anybody ever gave me. He said, and I quote, "Simon, you're a tough son of a bitch."

Unions

I look back with great fondness on all my union experiences – even those early terrifying ones. I had earlier union interactions with a play called *Tobacco Road*. It didn't require any props; the actors just went out on the bare stage and did it. There was a group of the trades: carpenters, electricians, and property – heads of department they were called. But the union had the three heads of department plus other union people sitting down under the stage playing cards all during the play's run of several years. And these guys just sat there getting paid for playing cards.

These guys came to see me one day in my Carnegie office. They were big guys, 200-pounders or more, and they used 4-letter words. That's hard for you to imagine because children do it today without batting an eye, but no one did in those days; I'd hardly ever heard anybody use them. So this was a fairly terrifying experience, having these guys insisting we pay for three heads of department. We needed them like a hole in the head. We were having a really tough time making the mortgage payments. So I, quavering in my boots, said I was sure the newspapers would enjoy the story of their closing down Carnegie Hall for this holdup. They walked away; that was the end of it. This was quite a relief.

Carnegie Recital Hall

The creation of the Recital Hall was the most memorable part of my Carnegie experience. Before then, Town Hall served as the debut concert hall, with 1,400 seats and a poor acoustic system. This was not the best situation for a debut recitalist playing for friends and relatives. I got the idea that this could be a great boon for new recitalists looking to debut and for Carnegie Hall.

We started by closing up some windows to remove traffic noise. Then we went on to get regular theatrical seats rather than the Bentwood chairs, we enlarged the stage, and fixed the lighting. It became apparent that just like athletes needed a place to visit before the event, so did artists – but there was no john there. So one day we were moping around trying to find a place. We had just about given up when the light dawned as we passed the entrance to the second floor corridor to the Concert Hall. Here was this huge wall and a door. Carnegie Hall was not a steel structure; it was solid brick, so

"I got the idea that this could be a great boon for new recitalists looking to debut and for Carnegie Hall."

we had our mason chisel out a cave in the wall. We brought the plumbing in and created a bathroom. We produced various concerts, but the critics wouldn't come and that's no good for a debutante. Since I couldn't persuade them, I went to see Arthur Sulzberger Sr., publisher of the *New York Times*. I persuaded him to assign his critics to cover the debuts. Then it blossomed exponentially. From that we built some handsome spaces for audiences to congregate and dressing rooms.

Corridors of Carnegie Hall

Musicians, painters, dancers, and actors thrived in the two towers built by 19th-century industrialist Andrew Carnegie just after the Hall went up in 1891. The towers, often referred to as the Corridors, housed more than 100 studios and apartments, some with special skylights installed to give painters the northern light they prized.

The **Corridors** of Carnegie Hall were just fabulous. There were artists living and working there. They had studios there. We modernized as we went along. The 57th Street building has higher ceiling heights than the 56th Street building. So as a

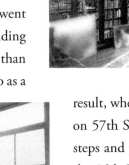

result, when you get to the 6th floor on 57th Street, you walk up 6 or 7 steps and you're on the 8th floor of the 56th Street building. As you get off the elevator on 57th Street, the first thing you run into is Studio 61. That was a huge dance studio where *Oklahoma!* was staged, where Agnes de Mille, Isadora Duncan, Twyla Tharp, and others shared the space. The fun there would be to see all the ballet people doing their plies and hearing the vocal students doing their thing.

Agnes de Mille captured the spirit of the Corridors by remarking, "Everyone was working very hard. Sometimes it was banging; sometimes it was real talent. But under our feet was Toscanini, who was like a steady hand to the back that said, 'Keep going, do your best.' "

The list of luminaries who inhabited the Corridors is impressive and varied: author Norman Mailer, singer Bobby Short, and dancer Isadora Duncan. Mark Twain and Theodore Roosevelt smoked cigars by the fireplace in the Author's Club; Martha Graham established her first dance studio; Enrico Caruso made his first recordings in America; Lucille Ball took voice coaching; Leonard Bernstein composed music; and Joe Raposo wrote songs for *Sesame Street*. Marilyn Monroe, Grace Kelly, and Robert Redford took acting lessons; James Dean memorized scripts. A particularly favored tenant, Marlon Brando, took refuge with a neighbor when overzealous fans discovered they could climb the stairs to his apartment unimpeded. To demonstrate his gratitude, Brando sent her a dozen roses with this note attached: "In appreciation for courageous perseverance displayed in Hall Battling and Neighborliness above and beyond the call of duty." He signed it "Not so Private Citizen, Marlon Brando." He'd go on to win the Academy Award for *On the Waterfront* while living in the Corridors. And, while not officially a tenant, and not yet known by her Hollywood name, Joan Crawford began her career dancing on the tables in the basement speakeasy.

In 2010, Carnegie Hall converted the 150 apartments into much needed backstage, rehearsal, and music education spaces. Bob was one of the first to tour the renovations in 2013 and enthusiastically approved of what he considered a beautifully designed education center.

World War II

It was 1941 when Pearl Harbor hit. It took me a little while to realize that I had to get involved because I couldn't see myself not being involved. I went down to Lower Manhattan to sign up as a volunteer. They sent me to a camp in Long Island, an induction center. I was issued my clothes and went to the barracks. The first day I was on a detail, KP[15] or something. A fellow soldier told me that was a stupid thing to do; he told me all I had to do was hide in the bushes and let everybody else do it. I followed his good advice for about three weeks.

I met a lot of people I never would have met. I'll never forget one guy who had never had shoes on in his life. He put on his socks and the rest of his uniform and put his shoes over his shoulder and walked out.

In those days, four-letter words were never used with the groups I went with. Here they were used as a sign of manhood. At the mess table the guys would say, "Pass me the fucking bread." They just said it all the time to bolster their courage. They were quite scared, these guys. As a matter of fact, at the induction center, we were all naked lined up going for our shots and the guys who had gone before would yell out, "Watch out for the big one," describing the needles. One of them passed out cold when he got the shot. Many of them had never had a shot before.

We were lined up to sign things. When it came to signing papers, I was used to this: I'd been signing leases for eight years. In New York I was negotiating leases with lawyers at my side. And here we were being asked to sign papers: just step up to the table and sign here. You'd have been absolutely queer in the old sense of the word if you'd insisted on reading the papers.

---

[15] Kitchen patrol. Work assigned to junior enlisted military personnel.

Fort Lee, Virginia

The day came when my name was called; I was to be shipped out to Fort Lee, Virginia. We got there in the early hours of the morning because whenever any important train – the ones carrying goods – came through, we were sidetracked; we were just people. They took us to the mess hall. That was the first time I'd ever seen hominy grits. I didn't like them too much at 2:00 in the morning. I've learned to like them since.

I did three months of basic training. The first day the drill instructor asked our full names. When I gave mine he asked, "What does the 'E' stand for?" "Edward, sir!" "Well, fuck you, Edward!" It went on like that.

Then followed three months as an acting corporal with a squad to take care of, and three months at Officer Candidate School at Fort Lee. I really enjoyed it very much. I had had more responsibility than was good for someone my age when I was 21, 22, and here I didn't have to decide what to put on, when to get up, when to go to bed, nothing. I didn't have to decide a single thing. It was wonderful, very relaxing.

I loved doing the close-order drills. At night, I'd conjure up formations and I'd try them out on my squad the next day. I would send them out to the four winds and see if I could get them back together. I loved it. It was fun. Of course if I goofed that was even more fun.

At Camp Lee, we learned to fire a rifle. The difference between the US forces and the others, all our guys knew how to pick a target and hit it at 200 yards rather than just shooting blindly. I got a sharpshooter medal, which is not the best one. An amusing thing is I can't close one eye.

On Christmas Eve, I was "Charge of Quarters," which meant I had to sit in the lieutenant's office and answer the phone if anything happened. The lieutenant came in and dropped off his wife and went on to the party. She was feeling pretty miserable, so I tried to cheer her up. We talked and sang Christmas carols together. So there I was, an acting corporal, with my feet on the lieutenant's desk and she was sitting next to me and we were singing when this jackass came in. He was absolutely fit to be tied that she was having a relationship with an enlisted man. I don't think that marriage lasted much longer.

I used to go to a town on the James River within walking distance of Fort Lee. There were two old ladies with a sign on their picket fence that said, "Welcome Servicemen." So I went in one day and many times thereafter I returned to spend the weekend. I'd work their garden for them and they fed me. It was lovely. They were great. It was a home away from home.

One day I put on my dress uniform, dress shoes, and went for a walk. I came back and realized I had walked 22 miles. The conditioning was such that it was nothing. I asked my wife[16] to bring down the squash shorts I had worn in college, and they fit!

Bob and his mother Elsa.

[16] Helen. Bob's wife from 1939 until her death in 1959.

Kansas City Quartermaster Depot

After graduation I was assigned first to the Kansas City Quartermaster Depot and then to automotive school in Omaha, Nebraska. I'm not a mechanical type, but I am a good student. I learned what they taught. In the final exam, they screwed up a jeep engine and I had to fix it. After that, if any of my friends had a problem with their car I'd say, "Stand back," and I'd get in there and fix it. Today I can barely find the engine because it doesn't come naturally to me.

Harvard Business School

The Army sent me to Harvard Business School for three months as part of the first quartermaster class there. The Air Force had been there for some time. What used to drive us crazy is that they'd have parades every so often. The Air Force didn't know the first thing about close-order drill or anything else, and they'd go slopping down the street singing "Off We Go Into the Wild Blue Yonder." These were accountants, and guys like that were not going to see the sky very much. The crowd would go bananas over that. Then we'd come along in pretty good shape. The highlight was when Winston Churchill came to speak. He was a great orator.

How Bob Won the War

When people wonder who won the war, well, I'm here to tell you, it was I. Before I got there, the baseball equipment was being delivered in the fall and the football equipment in the spring. It was terrible for morale. So I wrote a letter and I sent it down for the depot commander's signature. He sent it on through the proper channels. After a few months, a letter came back to the depot commander thanking him for his brilliant suggestion, which would be implemented. The depot commander was a chicken colonel.[17] My boss, who was a major, was fit to be tied; he wanted the credit so he demoted me. So, at this point, I applied to go overseas. I spent the three weeks prior to my deployment in grave registration. It was part of my punishment.

Shipping Out

I was told I was needed in Europe. So a group of us flew to Prestwick, Scotland, and then boarded a train to London where they put us up in the center of town. I had made a couple of friends by the time we left. Jack Moran was a very handsome, blue-eyed Irish type. St. Germain was an IBM guy. His devotion to IBM impressed me. They really had a religion going on at that time. Wherever we went, he wanted to see if there was an IBM office there.

We dropped our bags and headed for Piccadilly – that's where all the action was. We wanted to see what the blackouts were like. As we were standing there in front of a building in the pitch dark, two GIs came out of one door and two female Brits came out another one. "Well, that was short and sweet," the girls remarked.

These two Army friends of mine were absolutely uncultured, so I made it my job to change that as much as I could. I initiated one GI after another into the business of eating snails. At that time, I thought it was my mission to teach them.

We went to the theater often. One of the shows was *Thanks, Yanks*, starring Hermione Gingold. Not long after, I went into a real estate office one day, just to see how they worked. In waltzed Hermione. I had forgotten her name. So I went up to her and I said, "I thought you were terrific in *Thanks, Yanks*." She invited me to her dressing room and then she invited me to her friend Lady Brown's house. The happening band in London at the moment

---

[17] A full colonel as opposed to a lieutenant colonel.

rehearsed in her ballroom because their usual site had been bombed out. They invited me to a dance. We Yanks had soap; they didn't. I danced with this heavenly Welsh girl, and by God it was an experience of the senses!

I remember discussions with the British; I learned the protocol system they used so effectively. They'd guess who was going to be on the American team – the rank or importance of the participants. If we had a major, they'd have a general, even if that general had just a temporary rank. There were many "generals for a day."

Denmark

They sent me up to Denmark to straighten out a purchasing mess. I tried to get a lift up there and I spent several days without success. I got a hold of a Navy goose[18] that was headed that way. I got there New Year's Eve and I learned how to say Happy New Year in Danish: "Godt Nytår." The Danes were wonderful. I was in uniform and people would come up to me in the street and thank me. I met a woman who brought me to her family – we had meals with mama, papa, and her kid sister. There I learned the virtue of Akvavit.[19] They use it in a boilermaker: a straight shot of Akvavit and beer. It's made in rough bars by rough people.

I make a Danish Mary with Akvavit. I persuaded bars in New York to carry it. If you special order it, they'll have it in two weeks. Now you can get it all over Lake Anne.[20] A friend of mine and I tried to become the Virginia importers but the company said, "No thanks" – but they did send special Akvavit glasses! The big thrill of Denmark was that I got to eat butter, eggs,

[8] Amphibious aircraft.
[9] A Danish flavored spirit and essential ingredient in Bob's Danish Mary cocktail.
[20] Lake Anne Plaza in Reston, Virginia.

and milk. When I got everything settled, I moved on to Stockholm. The Swedes were mostly rooting for the Germans.[21] No one thanked me for anything or invited me to dinner. I stayed at the Grand Hotel where half the dining room was for the Allies, the other half was for the Germans. Soon we had VE Day.

Brussels

When we were billeted in Brussels I looked around the quarters and saw a mirror on the ceiling and a bidet. I soon realized where they had put us – in a maison de rendez-vous! We were supposed to be able to bathe by appointment only, but the owner gave his customers the tub room – we never got to use it. The johns were in an open courtyard with an air raid siren on the roof. It wasn't too long before the siren went off while I was out there.

Returning Home

When it came time to go home, I was hoping to go to Czechoslovakia. I ended up in a chateau in Le Havre[22] waiting for ships to take us home. I was in charge of German POWs. We had a chamber orchestra comprised of POWs. After three weeks of that high living we got on the troop transport ship to take us home.

They dumped us in a camp in New Jersey. My mother and sisters came out for a family reunion. It had been three years. We got into a donnybrook – a big fight. I told them the Russians were not our allies at all, rather co-combatants. The Russians relabeled the supplies we sent them so the people handling it didn't know it came from us. The most important thing was that they were fortifying their furthest, most advanced positions, against all agreements. They were digging in. I said we should tell them that we thought

---

[21] Sweden remained neutral in World War II.
[22] French port city where the Seine River meets the English Channel.

they'd made a mistake, that they should get back into Russia where they belonged; if they didn't, we'd hit them with an atom bomb. Leave Hungary, Czechoslovakia alone. My family had a fit because the Russians were our dearest friends and they knew it.

Syosset

I came back from the war to a new apartment that I had never seen. In addition, there was Paul Simon,[23] whom my wife Helen had adopted while I was in the Army. It wasn't too long before Helen and I moved to Syosset, Long Island. In 1947 we got Margo from the same adoption agency. Our home on Split Rock Road was no great shakes, but it sat on five beautiful acres. There were a couple of houses nearby. In one direction there was a house with a girl Margo's age; in the other direction was a boy a couple years older than Paul. That was it. There we were on five acres with two children. I commuted into the city. The experience of having to drive these two kids everywhere made my wife a very unhappy lady.

Skating

The kids and I got into figure skating. I took them to be fitted for skates at what turned out to be the best skate store there was in Greater New York. After the purchase we started out the door and the salesman said to me, "If those skates don't work for the kids, bring them back. It will be my fault, not theirs." This made an impression. As a kid, Manhattan was so cold in the

---

[23] Not the musical partner of Art Garfunkel.

winter that they'd flood the tennis courts at 122nd and Riverside Drive with a hose to make an ice rink – no refrigeration needed. We'd buy season passes. I spent the time skating around on my ankles: the skates weren't fitted right. My parents would buy the skates three sizes too big so I'd grow into them. I'd never skated properly at all.

So I ended up buying skates for myself as well. I really got into it. Sixteen of us put on an ice dancing show at the end of the year, to the mortification of the club members. One of the most sublime moments of my life was when, as a club, we invited the third-ranked ice dancing pair to put on a performance on a Saturday night. Then on Sunday, they came and skated with the 16 of us. I got to skate with the third-ranked lady in the USA. Let me tell you, doing these dances I'd worked so hard to learn with this lady – well, I was good! My partner had been a rather stout lady whose husband figured we must have something going on, so he bought skates and joined our skating group.

Into the Sound

One of the great memories is being on the boat with Margo when a fog came down on us. We were coming out of the river and when we got under the bridge and out into the sound we couldn't see a damn thing. The waves were such that we weren't making any headway. I became very concerned; we had a compass, but no other modern conveniences. So Margo was sitting with her back to the side, braced there as we went up and down, up and down. The anchor broke loose and I said, "You've got to get up there and secure the anchor." She did. While I was wondering if we'd ever get home, she said, "I'm hungry." She jumped down the hatch, made a peanut butter sandwich, and ate it, as I was worried about surviving the storm.

Levittown

It was sometime in this period that I first visited Levittown. I'd often heard about this postwar phenomenon – over 20,000 veterans and their families housed in 750 square foot, look-alike, single-family homes. Levittown was known to be "the pits." This was unchallenged by my friends and acquaintances. But I didn't think so. The Levittown that I saw on my visit was thriving: it was teeming with kids playing in cul-de-sacs. They were having a hell of a time playing in the streets. I wondered if these families were having a better time than mine. This time on Long Island was very important to me in terms of what I wanted to do in Reston. I saw all these women stuck at home. Two-income, working families were not as common then as they are today. The women were chauffeurs. They just drove their kids around and went crazy. This had a significant impact on my goals for Reston.

Downtown Staten Island

Staten Island – that was a good one. It was the most glamorous one outside of Reston. I bought an abandoned airport right out in the middle of the island. There was a farmer's market on it – a big operation, seven days a week. At that time, Manhattan was connected to Staten Island only by a ferry, not by a bridge, and there was only one business district area, right by the ferry. With the forecast for increased population, it seemed inevitable that the center would move to a more central location – to our airport. The property we bought was right in the center of the island and it was well located in terms of the highways.

I got a hold of Victor Gruen. He was the father of the regional shopping center and the father of the closed-to-vehicular-traffic, pedestrian-access shopping streets. I asked Victor for help with the master plan. This was a substantial piece of land – well over 100 acres. What we came up with was a regional shopping center with a couple of department stores and some mid-rise and high-rise apartments. We were calling it Downtown Staten Island. At the time, this was no place at all, but the plans, elevations, and drawings that Gruen did were impressive. We got the borough president to display our plans in his office. The thing began to look promising. We started selling at $5,000 an acre and ended up at $14,000 an acre. Financially, we did very well with that. But we didn't build anything: we sold it off piece by piece.

In the course of negotiations, Federated Department Stores sent in a guy named Jim Selonick. I was so impressed by him that after that project I decided I wanted him on my side. He became executive vice president of Simon Enterprises and would come with me to Reston.

Sale of Carnegie Hall

Bob's father proposed selling Carnegie Hall to the New York Philharmonic in the early 1930s, but Philharmonic Chairman Marshall Field rejected the below-market offer because the Hall lacked facilities, namely air conditioning and restrooms. Having made significant improvements since his father's tenure, Bob picked up the idea.

It seemed to me ridiculous for private people to own Carnegie Hall. I felt the Philharmonic could benefit from owning it. There had been talks of building new concert halls in the past and it didn't make a lot of sense for our private company to be operating this international institution. I felt Carnegie Hall should be in public or quasi-public hands. I worked through a variety of people in the hierarchy.

I had many conversations with Arthur Judson. He was the great king of classical music in his time, representing the major conductors, orchestras, and soloists through his management company. And he was manager of the Philadelphia Orchestra. People weren't paying much mind to the conflict of interest there. His assistant, Bruno Zirato, had risen from Caruso's ballet to this position of number-two man to Judson. He later became executive

"I felt Carnegie Hall should be in public hands."

director of the New York Philharmonic. And then there was a friend, Floyd Blair. He and I skated together in the country. He was vice president of First National City Bank in charge of entertaining foreign visitors, and he was president of the Philharmonic. At a variety of times I approached them to see if they would get organized to buy Carnegie Hall from us.

I think I told you about my relationship with Robert Moses.[24] He was the great power in New York City. He had determined that one of his great monuments would be Lincoln Center. I tried to persuade him that it was a dumb idea.

[24] Polarizing urban planner known as New York City's "Master Builder" for his mid-century public construction projects.

When Bob unexpectedly found himself in a cab with Moses, he seized the opportunity to give him the equivalent of a 30-second elevator pitch. Bob challenged, "If you could pick up the Paris Opera, Comédie Française, and Théâtre des Champs Élysées and put them in one place, do you think that would be a good idea?" Moses was unmoved.

In April of 1955, Moses announced his intent, under the auspices of Mayor Wagner's Slum Clearance Committee, to demolish 25 acres of tenements around Lincoln Square to make way for an arts center. He promised new buildings to the New York Philharmonic, Juilliard, and the Metropolitan Opera.

> **So I had a meeting** with Blair and Zirato, and Blair said the price we were quoting for Carnegie Hall was too high. That teed me off because we had always quoted what I thought was a quarter-million under market price. So I said to Blair, if my board will agree to it, we'll sign a contract with you that will give you a year to try to find the money to buy the Hall and the price will be arbitrated. When the Philharmonic turned that down, I knew we better get out as quick as we could. Without revenue from the Philharmonic, we couldn't even pay the water bill.

Save Carnegie Hall!

But Isaac Stern,[25] and the "Save Carnegie Hall" group that coalesced around him, calculated that a combination of the public-ownership tax-exempt status, aggressive fundraising, and innovation would allow the Hall to survive without the Philharmonic. In fact, the Philharmonic's departure literally made way for a lucrative revenue stream. In those days it took 48 hours to lay the enormous television cables needed for broadcast. The Philharmonic schedule – performances four nights a week plus rehearsals – left little time for the lengthy setup. This new flexibility began the era of profitable televised specials featuring the Emmy

---

[25] Celebrated violinist, conductor, and classical music power broker.

Awards, Ed Sullivan, Carol Burnett and Julie Andrews, Jack Benny, and even Captain Kangaroo.

I made a contract with real estate developer Louis J. Glickman to sell the Carnegie Hall properties for $5,250,000. The contract provided for cancellation of the transaction if a nonprofit or civic organization should be prepared to buy Carnegie Hall. Glickman retained architect Ralph Pomerance, who happened to be married to my sister-in-law – a wild coincidence. He designed a building that I though was stunning. Its red tile was designed to stand out in the Manhattan skyline. I thought it was a great design, but this was like a red flag in front of the bull; the public went absolutely berserk at the concept of this red building replacing Carnegie Hall.

In the end, we found a way to preserve Carnegie Hall for posterity by selling it to the City of New York, thus negating the contract with Glickman. With the agreement of my board, I set the price to the City at $5,000,000. It was our wish to make the $250,000 difference between what we had contracted and what the City would pay as our contribution in saving Carnegie Hall. This got lost in the Save Carnegie Hall movement that I started and that Isaac Stern led to glory.

In a letter to Isaac Stern dated January 8, 1981, Bob sought to set the record straight. He writes,

> You, Isaac, were the key factor in the "Save Carnegie Hall" movement – no question of that. But I was the founder of that movement. It all started with my calling John Totten, long time House Manager of Carnegie Hall – whom, I know you remember well. After Floyd Blair had turned down my proposal to sell Carnegie Hall to the Philharmonic at an arbitrated price, I described the situation to Totten and asked him to start a movement to save Carnegie Hall. I explained to him that my

involvement in the movement would, obviously, have to be kept secret because it would be so easy to misunderstand it. I told him of our Directors' approval of the $250,000 price differential. Thereafter, John and I worked together. We agonized together until the happy day when you, Isaac, were brought in to head the "Save Carnegie Hall" team. The rest is history, for which you and Vera deserve everlasting gratitude. But the past is history too. No reason to keep on perpetuating the myth that is so unflattering to the group I represent and to me. Why not from now on tell it as it was?

Bob goes on in the letter to encourage Isaac Stern to amend future accounts of the sale and the Save Carnegie Hall movement. He even provides recommended text. But there's no evidence Isaac Stern ever responded to Bob's letter.

Five years later, when Carnegie Hall's first (and current) archivist, Gino Francesconi, began looking, he found little documentation of the Simon family ownership era. So he began digging.

Gino discovered Bob's actions to support the effort including providing dedicated meeting space for the Committee to Save Carnegie Hall. Upon learning that Bob was still living, he went straight to the source to get the complete story.

Gino likes to say his initial inquires to Bob were met with "Stern" resistance. Gino persisted, ultimately winning Bob over with his earnest desire to uncover the truth. "If you want the truth," Bob replied, "I'm your man!" The ensuing collaboration allowed Gino to return Bob and his father to their proper place in Carnegie Hall history and to honor their legacy of stewardship, improvements, and innovations. Gino also had Bob's $250,000 donation to the Hall formally recognized with a plaque on the donor's wall.

Years later, while recording Vera Stern's[26] oral history, Gino asked her, "If you saw Bob Simon walking down the street, would you punch it out or shake

---

[26] Isaac Stern's wife from 1951-1994.

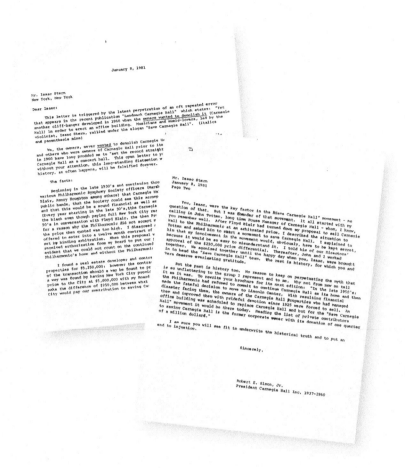

hands?" She replied, "You mean he's still among the living?" "Indeed, and kicking," answered Gino. Vera confirmed Gino's hypothesis, that Bob wasn't the villain in the Simon/Stern faceoff. Vera suggested having a lunch honoring Bob. When Gino informed Bob of the reconciliatory plans he exclaimed, "Leave it to a woman!" In July 2006 Gino reunited the three families so linked to Carnegie Hall: Andrew Carnegie's great-grandson Kenneth Miller; Isaac Stern's widow, Vera; and Bob. At lunch, Gino asked if it was true that during the Save Carnegie Hall campaign, Vera Stern knocked on his door one day and said, "You're just going to have to give us the hall!" Bob smiled and confirmed this story.

From early marketing materials.

Part 3: Reston

Buying the Land

After selling Carnegie Hall for $5 million, I was looking to invest the $2 million that remained[27] in like property[28] when I was approached by Jimmy Salkeld. He was the leading broker in Washington. His chief claim to fame was that he had lunch once a week with J. Edgar Hoover, the head of the FBI. He came to New York to sell property bought by Smith Bowman in 1925. Now dead, his two sons Smith and Delong Bowman inherited the land and sold it to Lefcourt Realty. Lefcourt got into financial trouble soon after buying this property and offered it back into the market. So the broker, Jimmy Salkeld, went to New York to try to sell it to Roger Stevens.[29] Roger Stevens wasn't interested in the acreage, let alone the distillery. Looking to amortize his $32 round trip airfare, Salkeld asked a Stevens associate for a lead on a likely customer. The associate got in touch with Henry Rice, a good friend of mine. Henry Rice knew I was looking for investment property and Jimmy Salkeld told a persuasive story. The property, less the distillery and its surrounding land, consisting of 6,750[30] acres could be had on unusually favorable terms. It was deal of a lifetime, he said:

> "You can buy the 6,750 acres for $8,000,000 down. The $12 million mortgage will be interest free for ten years. You'll recoup the down payment the first year -- I have a customer ready to buy one of the four intersections of the Dulles Access road to be built and there is an outer circumferential highway to be built."

[27] Bob paid out $3 million to non-family investors.
[28] To avoid capital gains tax.
[29] New York real estate magnate, legendary Broadway producer, and chairman of the John F. Kennedy Center for the Performing Arts.
[30] Later increased to 7,500 acres.

That sounded too good to ignore – a huge transaction that could be accomplished without any cash outlay. So I flew to DC, rented a jeep, and headed out to get the lay of the land. It was attractive, beautiful land. Half of it was woods and half pasture. There were 3,000 cattle grazing at the moment. They were not only eating grass, but they were consuming the mash from the distillery. These were happy steers and cows.

But it didn't take me too long to see there was no imminent outer-circumferential highway.[31] This made the recoupment of the initial cash investment ridiculous. When I became convinced that there was no outer-circumferential highway on the ground, let

"These were happy steers and cows."

alone in any of the plans, I wondered if there was to be an airport. I managed to get up to fencing beyond which I could see big Cats[32] scratching the ground out there. That was to be the airport. So now driving on dirt roads, walking through fields and seeing the woods persuaded me that it would be exciting as well as wise to take on this fabulously located offering. It was midway between our nation's capitol and its future airport.

We signed the contract and took title in 1961. It was the largest commitment I had made in the 26 years since I took over my family's real estate business.

Bob's stepdaughter, Lynn Lilienthal, recalled "I remember Bob trying to explain what this place would be like, showing us drawings and maps, but to us up in New York, it was always far away in Virginia."

[31] The Fairfax County Parkway would be built 25 years later.
[32] Caterpillar earth-moving equipment.

Dreaming

I had a few months to start planning what to do with this property. Uppermost in my mind was to create a community. We should use this opportunity to build more than just another suburban subdivision. I wanted to avoid creating a suburbia, where, as Gertrude Stein described, "There is no there there." I pulled out a yellow pad and started working on a preliminary development plan. I listed everything I had seen or read about that I could think of that made living stimulating and worthwhile. My list was inclusive. I paid no regard to practicality. I crossed out items that didn't suit the topography or climate of Northern Virginia. But, in the winter of 1966, Reston experienced a tremendous snowfall. One of the items I'd eliminated from my list was skiing. But now, I realized this had been a mistake. There was a really steep hill behind the dam we'd built to collect water for Lake Anne. No urging was needed for us to spring into action. We installed a donkey engine at the base of the slope and a rope tow leading to the top. We painted a sign "Mt. Reston – Elevation 187 feet" and awaited the coming of the more adventurous citizens. They came!

Live, Work, and Play

Early Reston employee Jane Wilhelm remembered,

"The years that I worked here were just like the first years of the Kennedy administration. These first years of Reston were Camelot. It was so exciting. Everyone who worked here was totally dedicated to the whole thing. It was a fascinating, new idea and everything was possible."

We threw out ideas – everything and anything was on the table. From that evolved these 7 goals:

1. That the widest choice of opportunities be made available for the full use of leisure time. This means that the New Town should provide a wide range of cultural and recreational facilities as well as an environment for privacy.

2. That it be possible for anyone to remain in a single neighborhood throughout his life, uprooting being neither inevitable nor always desirable. By providing the fullest range of housing styles and prices – from high-rise efficiencies to 6-bedroom townhouses and detached homes – housing needs can be met at a variety of income levels and at different stages of family life. This kind of mixture permits residents to remain rooted in the community – if they so choose – as their particular housing needs change. As a by-product, this also results in the heterogeneity that spells a lively and varied community.

3. That the importance and dignity of each individual be the focal point for all planning, and take precedence over large-scale concepts.

4. That the people be able to live and work in the same community.

5. That commercial, cultural, and recreational facilities be made available to the residents from the outset of the development – not years later.

6. That beauty – structural and natural – is a necessity of the good life and should be fostered.

7. Since Reston is being developed from private enterprise, in order to be completed as conceived it must also, of course, be a financial success.

The 7th goal was the most misunderstood – that it be economically success-ful. This is not a hierarchy saying that the 1st is the most important and the 7th the least important. What was clear in my head was that if this were not a very big success economically, it would be a waste of time. I used to say to the cluster groups[33] if Rockefeller gave Reston to the world, it would be the only one. That's not the idea; this thing has to be viable for anyone to want to do it again.

Inspiration

We looked to the British Isles for the big picture. After WWII they embarked on a program of building "New Towns." New Towns was the term d'art for the movement inspired by their Garden City movement the previous century. We'd taken a leaf out of that movement with Radburn, New Jersey – my fa-ther had been on the Board of Radburn but the Depression thwarted that. It wasn't until we came along that the New Town movement resurged.

We also looked to cities such as New York, Philadelphia, and Boston for their townhouses and Europe and South America for their plazas. Plazas are social – where people gather informally, exchange gossip, sip wine in bistros, observe the passing scene. It's hard to account for the paucity of plazas in America. We planned plazas for every village center and at least one in the Town Center. Retail would be conducted on ground floors above which there'd be residential.

[33] Neighborhood associations.

Tapiola Influence

There is nothing new here in Reston except the collection of things. It is eclectic. In Tapiola, a New Town outside of Helsinki, they had the good sense to build on top of a subway station.[34] The main feature of the town was a high-rise office building. If we built an office building, it could be vacant for years, if we built a residential building we could fill it up if the rent was low enough. I like there to be a focal point – if you've had too much to drink you can find your way home.

Heron House, Lake Anne Plaza.

Simon City

I wanted the name of our New Town to have a relationship to me while letting people be in on the joke. Back at home in New York they liked to tease me and call my project "Simon City." We all found it wonderfully repulsive. As I recall, it was a Friday afternoon and Fairfax County told us they needed a name by Monday. We were on Martha's Vineyard. My wife Anne[35] and my mother debated possible names. Neither was a shrinking violet. The PR firm sent someone up to the Vineyard to make a presentation on the name and, you guessed it, they suggested Simon City. I said, "You've got to be kidding." That was obviously repugnant. My mother and wife came up with Reston by using my initials plus "ton" and I liked it. This gave me and my family pleasure without insulting the people who live there.

---

[34] Many years later, Bob returned to Tapiola to revisit the source of his inspiration. He was nonplussed to find that while there was a subway system in Helsinki, it did not extend to Tapiola.
[35] Bob's wife from 1960–1971 for whom Lake Anne was named.

Planning Reston

When we got rolling on planning Reston I had a fairly busy office in New York and I thought it would be a good idea to have a super guy in charge down here in Virginia. Through a headhunter, I found Mike DiSalle, who was ex-governor of Ohio. After interviewing him and getting his absolute assurance he'd do this full time, I brought him in. He turned up with an aide by the name of Jim Malone. His idea was that Jim Malone would do the work and he'd be free to do his politicking in Ohio and the other things he enjoyed doing.

I think one of the more amusing moments of my entire life was when I went to Pennsylvania to meet a great tycoon in real estate, whose name I forget. Why I went to see him, I don't remember. At any rate, I went with

Mike DiSalle. The tycoon had an ex-governor as his aide. So there we were, two guys sitting down with our ex-governors. His was the ex-governor of Pennsylvania. I wasn't happy with what Mike was doing so I let him go. I moved down here myself and moved into the Bowman House. Jim Selonick came down as executive VP here. He was terrific, wonderful.

Jim shared similar feelings about his time in Reston:

"Robert Simon and Reston proved to be the most exhilarating and psychically rewarding work experience of my lifetime. Forget the frequent necessary decisions about which of our creditors were to be paid; forget the regular trips to the moneylenders at 14% interest; forget the shocking turndown for financing by a major life insurance company in New York because Bob insisted on building an integrated community in Virginia."

Then the question was how to get organized. I hired Bartholomew, the largest planning organization in the country, to help plan the property. I forget how I got tied in with Ira "Dutch" Willard. He was the city manager of Miami and available to come back to his native Virginia. Dutch Willard was our first employee; he recruited Glenn Saunders, then city manager of Fairfax.

We started to build a support system of attorneys; we thought we should have someone who would appeal to the old Virginia group – that was Armistead "Army" Boothe. He was an Oxford graduate who had the oars of his scull in his office in Alexandria. He was there for atmosphere and overall influence. Then we had Ed Pritchard who was a journeyman lawyer who would be helpful with the New York attorneys. We had a political lawyer, Lytton Gibson, a real character. And I was able to get close to our Hunter Mill supervisor. He gave me his three telephone numbers – his home, office, and girlfriend. He also sold insurance. So I decided I had to buy a little insurance from him. But just a little – it was very expensive.

We had our New York attorneys working on governance and researching everything there was to research from Hawaii to Maine. Bartholomew didn't work out so well, I wasn't in sync with them. So I tried another firm that I should have thought of first: Conklin + Rossant. They had done the New Towns that I knew about: Radburn in New Jersey, and Greenbelt, Maryland. So these were the major players we had. Planners, lawyers, architects. Then we started to build staff.

Reston Staff

I hired Jane Wilhelm. She was one of the very earliest people we brought in. She came from the school bureaucracy. It was an act of great courage on her part. She was leaving a secure lifetime position with pensions and things you get with civil service. She was here to be in charge of social planning.

Jane reminisced,

"A friend called me about a man from New York working on a development in Fairfax County. Soon after I got a call from Bob Simon asking if I'd like to work in Reston. I drove down from McLean to Reston. Route 7 was still a narrow, two-lane road. Tyson's Corner was a small crossroads with a beer tavern and a vet. But it was beautiful. There were big dairy farms, a wheat field that waved in the wind. We met in Bob's executive office, an old white frame farmhouse on Spring Street in Herndon. He needed somebody to help expedite the formation of community facilities and

Jane Gilmer Wilhelm, Reston's Director of Community Relations, is here shown in the Lake Anne Community Center. Mrs. Wilhelm is also Executive Director of The Reston, Virginia Foundation for Community Programs,

help to get public schools, churches, and community centers operating in Reston before the people were ready to move in and still be near them.

I had never known people who worked as hard and long as Bob and his associates. He wasn't easy to work for because he always wanted more for Reston than anyone was capable of producing. But he was always exhilarating, imaginative, creative, and carried himself with style and flair. It was fun to go to work and see our progress. We had a bulletin board at the intersection of Village Road and Baron Cameron Avenue. The sales office had to get there early on Monday mornings and post the population count. It started at 114."

The Admiral

The two ladies[36] in the office were not working together well. Then I got the bright idea of having someone come in to handle them. I picked a fellow who was a retired admiral, he'd been a submariner in the war. He only encountered the enemy once. When he did, he went to the bottom, turned everything off, and waited for them to go away. Of course, I'm not the least bit knowledgeable

---

[36] Jane Wilhelm and Carol Lubin.

about naval affairs, but that's not the way one imagines intrepid submariners doing their thing. It turned out he wasn't able to handle these two ladies either; they were too much for him.

I decided to give the admiral something to do to restore his confidence. Here we had Lake

Artist's rendering of Lake Anne Plaza.

Anne, it was just starting to fill up. Not long before I'd been standing in the valley and through my open legs was running a little stream. I asked the crew, "Is this little stream going to create a lake?" They assured me it would. So I asked the admiral, what are we going to do to make it fun? Are we going to have something like the swan boat in Boston or sailboats all over the place? He started peppering me with detailed questions about capacity and outboard motors and God knows what. Literally, he was asking me detailed questions about things

"He told me it wouldn't be possible to sail a boat on Lake Anne."

he was supposed to know about. That was very discouraging. He told me because of the lay of the land, it wouldn't be possible to sail a boat on Lake Anne. That was very disappointing to me. Of course, as we know, that turned not to be accurate. I had to let him go, but not before he got me choice seats to the Kennedy inauguration. We sat together in the grandstand. That's when I found out about the submarine.

Priscilla Ames and Embry Rucker

No history of Reston would be complete without me telling you about Priscilla Ames and Embry Rucker. Priscilla joined staff in the early days to become the director of the Community Center on Lake Anne Plaza. Her mission was to welcome newcomers, introduce them to all the opportunities Reston had to offer, and refer those in need to the agency best equipped to help. She was an ombudsperson as well as a booking agent. If you wanted to use a community space you had to go through her. If you had trouble with your children or your husband you went to her. She knew all the families and was helpful to many of them in need of guidance. She stood at my side at all public functions, cueing me in on the names and proclivities of each person we were there to meet.

Embry arrived in Reston, an Episcopalian minister sent to build a church and a congregation in this New Town. He hadn't been here long when he reported back he wasn't going to build a church; all of Reston would be his church. Embry ministered to the many who came to him for solace and guidance.

Embry Rucker and Priscilla Ames stock shelves in the Lake Anne Grocery Store, scheduled to open tomorrow

Tiny Store to Aid Village Hungry for a Grocery

He set up an informal teen center, the Common Ground. When Lake Anne's supermarket moved out, thinking of the frustration of the seniors living across the way in the Fellowship House, he and Priscilla set up a small co-op grocery store. They were pioneers and activists and two of the very best.

Bowman House

My wife Anne and I lived in Delong Bowman's former house except weekends when I went back to New York. Smith Bowman, the older brother had a house nearby that later became Prison Fellowship.[37] A black couple, Norris and Rudeen, worked for us. Norris was a retired Navy type who had risen to chef of the admiral of the fleet. When they came into port, Norris commandeered a helicopter to do his shopping.

One of my favorite stories was when Anne asked Norris if he had ever cooked Shashlick. Norris said, "No, I've never cooked shashlick, but I have caused it to be cooked." Norris had had chefs under him to do the cooking. Breakfasts were served by Rudeen, whose portliness bespoke of her appreciation of her husband's culinary talents. Breakfast meetings were very popular at the Bowman House because eggs Benedict and Bloody Marys were often served. We had no problem getting people in for breakfast meetings.

Once a week we'd have meetings with the great impresario Patrick Hayes and his associate. We'd go over the plans and concepts that we had for bringing "cultcha" to our community.

Jane Wilhelm recalled,

"Bob wanted someone representing the arts in the area. The arts were sparse in DC in those years. I suggested Patrick Hayes. He was quite a character. He was an Irishman, a very good organizer, and a great reader of people. He started his own nonprofit called the Washington Performing Arts Society. He went straight to the top of the arts world in Washington. Bob decided to hire him as a consultant. He helped with all of our performing arts events."

---

[7] President Nixon's "hatchet man," Chuck Colson bought the property in the early 80s as the headquarters of his Prison Fellowship Ministries.

Fairfax County

Negotiating with Fairfax County for approvals proved to be the most delicate of tasks. In those days there were seven members of the board of supervisors.[38] I must tell you, six of these worthies were indicted for taking bribes and five served jail sentences.[39] I assure you, we in no way contributed to their embarrassment.

Bill Burrage was the head of the Fairfax County planning staff. There were 22 planners on staff. Bill Burrage was a Princeton graduate and he had a wife with champagne tastes, so he came to me and wanted to borrow $20,000 ($100,000 today). I declined the offer. I got a tape recorder and taped the conversation. So that was the group of County folks I had to deal with and Burrage was right in there with them.

Jane Wilhelm recollected,

"Bob was so aware of all the possibilities that he didn't make mistakes. He knew to be careful. He had come from New York to a rural county in Virginia and encountered and probably expected a governing board of supervisors and a civil service staff that weren't sophisticated at all, not too savvy. But there were a few that were. He had an absolute rule that could not be violated – anyone who gave a gift to an employee of Fairfax County or an elected official would be immediately fired. He knew that was a necessity. The old days in Virginia politics were as rotten as could be. Everything was bought with bribes. But he'd have none of it. He eventually got most of the things he wanted but it took longer because he wouldn't do anything that came anywhere near to a bribe."

---

[38] Today there are nine members.
[39] Fifteen county officials, developers, and zoning attorneys were indicted in a cash-for-zoning scandal. Eight were convicted in 1966 including three members of the board of supervisors.

VDOT

We had a Christmas Eve party at the Bowman House for the County and the highway superintendent from VDOT [Virginia Department of Transportation]. We'd been having a lot of trouble with him. So Glenn Saunders put us together in my bedroom with a drink in hand. We were talking about the size and topography of South Shore Drive. We had planned a gently rolling lane, serving those few detached houses. He was insisting on a super-highway cutting through the contours. At that historic meeting he said to me, "As far as I'm concerned, Reston ain't no different than a five-lot subdivision." I had held up the start of construction for three weeks, but after that I capitulated.

Residential Planned Community

Until challenged by Bob, Fairfax County adhered to the Department of Commerce's "Standard State Zoning Enabling Act," which provided a model used throughout the country and focused on separating incompatible uses. These conventional zoning ordinances segregated residential, industrial, and commercial uses. Bob believed these restrictions diffused communities into separate, unrelated areas that prevented the development of the community life he wanted for Reston. Bob and his team developed and proposed an innovative new code that incorporated his defining principles to allow residents to live, work, and play in the same community.

We developed the RPC[40] zoning. Our idea was to have it master planned apart from normal zoning. This was worked out with the County and our group. We had three of the County supervisors on our side as we approached

---

40 Residential Planned Community.

the July 1962 up or down vote on the new RPC ordinance and the master plan, but we didn't know about the other four. One of those who had helped us mightily at this point was Frederick "Fritz" Gutheim. He was the president for the Center for Metropolitan Studies. He successfully amended Kennedy's Year 2000 Plan that showed DC in the center and the radiation of the satellite cities planned around it. This was an important document and he managed to get Reston on the map – literally.

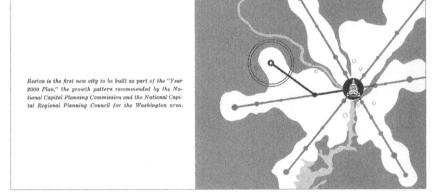

Reston is the first new city to be built as part of the "Year 2000 Plan," the growth pattern recommended by the National Capital Planning Commission and the National Capital Regional Planning Council for the Washington area.

Then Fritz went to work. In the week before the supervisors voted on our application, the *Washington Post* had seven articles, one of which was an editorial. The *Washington Star* had six articles, one of which was an editorial, and the Virginia press had headlines that looked like war had been declared. This was all Fritz's doing. Fritz was the world's preeminent scholar on this sort of thing. No one knew more about New Towns the world over than Fritz.

Hearing

We went to the hearing on July 15, 1962. I forgot to say that at one of the previous hearings after I had turned down Bill Burrage's request for a friendly loan, he changed his tune from being in favor of us to against us. At this particular hearing he turned up dead drunk. I asked Glenn Saunders to sit next to him and he did. The board of supervisors asked him questions and Glenn Saunders whispered answers in his ear.

The big deal at the hearing was school sites. We had held out on those but we were prepared to give in – which we did at the hearing. They wanted the sites for free and we wanted the County to pay for them. But we caved and that's what gave us the unanimous vote.

First Residents

When we opened up for sales, there were a lot of people who wanted to come here. This was the place to be. People came from the Midwest, etc. People came because they read all about it. The first who moved in here were terrific. This was a self-selected group of pioneers – they had bought

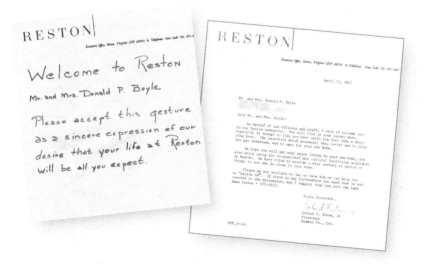

the publicity. Ten percent of our first buyers were single people; they wanted to be part of this thing. We were very concerned about what would happen after we had grown past the first village. How could we make it possible for them to share in the same kind of experience? We discussed it and decided to let them go it on their own.

At any rate, we sent each new resident a welcome letter and a basket of groceries so they wouldn't have to shop for three days. Milk, eggs, butter, staples. We did it because it was a welcoming thing and it prevented people from getting angry when the door handle fell off or something went wrong. I never did get a complaint; but I did get calls from people who perhaps had too much to drink at 1:00 in the morning.

Open Community

It would be hard to overestimate the boldness of Bob's Open Community mandate for Reston. In 1964, Virginia had yet to emerge from a period of civil rights abuses: institutionalized discrimination, lynchings, Senator Harry Byrd's massive resistance to integration, and the absence of fair housing laws. The strict segregation of neighborhoods went unchallenged.

The idea of community means people of all incomes and races living happily together. It was inconceivable that we'd do anything other than inclusiveness. So one of the things we said we'd do was have an open community – I'm under the impression that this was the first one in Virginia. We were turned down by 50 banks for normal construction loans. They were not interested in talking to us. The backers we did have were shocked and considered walking away from this thing.

We publicized that it was an open community. It wasn't the way they do it today with ads showing pictures of mixed groups. That would have been too tough in that market. But we did, otherwise they wouldn't come.

As Chuck Veatch notes in Rebekah Wingert-Jabi's excellent 2015 Reston documentary *Another Way of Living*, "This was a ripple in the fabric of what was then a very conservative northern Virginia."

Jane Wilhelm noted,

"This was the first integrated community built in Virginia. The law that prevented marriage and association between blacks and whites wouldn't be repealed until after Bob left. But here he was selling to blacks. He was undaunted. He had a rule that everyone who came to rent or buy was told that this was an open community. It should never happen that someone would move in and not know this."

The first black person to buy a lot in Hunters Woods was a lieutenant colonel in the Air Force. He had planned to build his own swimming pool. The next picked a lot across the street from the lieutenant colonel. My sales team came to me and said, "What are we going to do? We've got to tell him to move to another lot because nobody would believe that we didn't do this on purpose." We asked him to pick a different spot and that may have been the reason we never saw him again.

Jane Wilhelm recalled a similar situation:

"The first black family moved into Hunter Woods and then Heron House. It's amazing how little trouble there was. But some things did happen. I was the Director of Community Relations – it was my job to make sure everything ran smoothly. One Sunday morning I got a call. It was our public relations man, Bernie Norwitch. He said, 'You rented out an apartment above the Plaza[41] to a white family from Georgia and they are raising Cain over living next door to a black family. You better come up here.'

In those days, every family that moved in was presented with a basket of enough food for three meals. I think this couple would have been long gone if they hadn't received the basket. I knocked on the door and asked if they'd received their gift package. She said, 'Yes, we've eaten the first two meals and we're planning to eat the third one and get out of here.' I asked her, Now why would you do that? She said, 'We're from Georgia; we don't like living next to niggers.' I said, Well, that's understandable, being from Georgia. I told her that I had taught at the Georgia State College – her alma mater. So we began talking about our school, about Reston, and two hours went by. In the end, she said, 'You know, I guess we will stay and try it out.'"

---

[41]   Lake Anne Plaza. The first village center and neighborhood built in Reston.

Low-Income Housing

Bob Weaver[42] was very excited about the prospect of this New Town being built. He was influenced by the incredible flood of publicity. His praise for our efforts was tempered by his lamenting our failure to include any low-income housing. I told him we had enough to overcome – for one, being the first development of any size in Virginia to welcome people of all colors. Furthermore, local neighborhood realtors were known for discouraging their customers from looking at Reston, saying, "You don't want to go there – they're all communists!"

We needed time for the community to be ready to accept it. I told Weaver we planned to apply to his agency for a HUD [Housing and Urban Development] subsidy as soon as we'd become established. Finally came the time when the people were eager to have low-income housing as part of Reston. We applied for a Title VIII[43] loan on 240 units. Six months later, I got a letter from HUD saying our application was premature. I called Bob Weaver. He said, "Oh my God, I'll take care of that right away." He did not take care of it right away. It was after I left they concluded the deal for 120 units.

Binishells

Jane Wilhelm witnessed Bob's enthusiasm for bringing novel concepts to Reston. She recollected,

"Bob had so many ideas. He was interested in everything. But some things did not work out. He installed two charging stations for electric cars. He thought Reston would be the perfect place to introduce electric cars. He also got interested in this man who said he could solve the housing problems in Africa by building concrete houses."

---

[42] The first U.S. Secretary of Housing and Urban Development (HUD) and first African-American appointed to a cabinet-level position.
[43] Fair Housing Act.

Bob invited architect Dante Bini to demonstrate the formation of his low-cost, eco-friendly, domed concrete structures. Bob, HUD Secretary Weaver, and several Fairfax County officials looked on as Bini's team poured wet concrete upon an elastic membrane and then slowly inflated it to form the dome shape. Jane noted, "Unfortunately or probably fortunately, soon after they got the form all the way up the whole thing collapsed. But Bob never regretted any of that."

Architect Dante Bini's low-cost, eco-friendly, domed concrete structures.

Townhouses in the Boonies

Another thing that was different about our plan: townhouses in the boonies. This had been done since the beginning of time but not in the USA. In the hill towns of Italy there are townhouses in the boonies. The way the farmers in Italy and France and other countries did it was they'd have a community where they lived and they had a community where they'd farm.

But this was not the way the US did things. So the idea of townhouses in the boonies was considered a little weird. Residential on top of stores was not a popular concept. But the idea came from the Embarcadero in San Francisco. The great Mort Zuckerman [founder and chairman of real estate conglomerate Boston Properties] told me, "It took a lot of chutzpa for you to put those up there out in the boonies." The irony is that he has recently bought the Embarcadero where they're doing just that.

"Townhouses in the boonies was considered a little weird. Residential on top of stores was not a popular concept."

Jane recalled,

"People got so mad at him for putting shops under the apartments in Lake Anne. Folks who bought there were infuriated. They'd say, 'That's what we did in my hometown! People lived up over their stores because they were too poor to live anywhere else!' I spent a good part of many days calming residents down over things like this."

Three Flavors

Chuck Veatch, one of Bob's first townhome salesmen, remembers picking Bob up from National Airport and driving him by a development of traditional townhouses going up in Alexandria. "Why can't we build something like these?" Chuck asked. "Why would we do something that's already been done?" Bob replied.

We decided that we had to have three different flavors to give people a chance to find a compatible architectural style. We called the clusters vanilla, chocolate, and strawberry – something to suit everyone's taste. So rather than starting with just one, we started with three. The 90 townhouses in Waterview Cluster with pastel hues and tin roofs evoke a French fishing village. The 90 townhouses in

The new Smith townhouses

Planning, at Reston, also means variety. Beginning an entire city, from the beginning, should mean that one could find exactly the right kind of housing tailor-made to meet his family or individual needs. That is the Reston way. What one can't find in the fifty or more different townhouse floorplans, one can design or have designed as a detached home.

The interest expressed by homebuilders in the Reston concept has been encouraging. Already, over twenty separate builders are building or will soon build in Reston. Several of these custom-builders are already active in the townhouse field, others are offering single-family detached houses.

Hickory Cluster feel contemporary and urban. And the 47 townhouses in Washington Plaza are more classically urban.

One of my favorite remarks was made by a banker who said, "Bob, why in the hell are you doing 227 townhouses on spec, why don't you do one next to the sales center and see how they go?" We got so many turndowns that we thought possibly the bankers were right, so we decided to start Hunters Woods simultaneously with Lake Anne. That was a very expensive thing

to do – start another community with all the infrastructure required – sewers, roads, etc. But we thought we better do it because if we laid an egg up here in Lake Anne, we'd have something going in Hunters Woods. Hunters Woods offered detached single-family homes on one and two acres.

Village Centers

I wanted seven village centers and one town center. The question was, what was a village center? It was historically something with retail, residential, a church, and community stuff for the elderly and kids. That was our concept of the village center. Each village was to have a theme. The Hunters Woods theme was horses because Reston was close to Fauquier County and the Bowmans were great promoters of the Fairfax Hunt Club. The steeplechase was held each year on their land – now it's Baron Cameron Park.

Town Center

Creating a Town Center was very much in our minds. Conklin + Rossant did a wonderful design. Nevertheless and notwithstanding, I turned it down. I said, "This was not Reston, it would be fabulous in Rome, but it is much too much for us here." That whole area was supposed to feel like Georgetown with a dense urban core and lots of residential, and little local nodes of commercial. The reason why I had the architects design Lake Anne so it was unexpandable was to force us to start the Town Center.

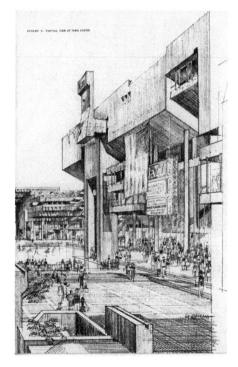

Artist's rendering of proposed Town Center.

"The Plaza used to fill up. They'd have photographers there to take a picture of the community. It was a big day for everybody."

Reston Festivals

The theory was when Reston was completed we'd have seven village centers. Each village center would have an annual festival and then the entire town would have a festival in the Town Center. For the Lake Anne festival we consulted the Smithsonian people for the best date in terms of rain. That took us to the third week in May. They were a lot of fun. We had no set formula for the festivals. One year, there were more guns than you could imagine. They had all kinds of military cadets and things. It had nothing to do with Reston. I expressed myself to the organizers. And the next year it was the children's festival and the kids were in the parade rather than the soldiers.

The Plaza used to fill up. They'd have photographers there to take a picture of the community. It was a big day for everybody. But in '72, there was this horrible, horrible happening. I was visiting Lynn Lilienthal.[44] I thought I'd go to the Plaza in the evening. When I got there it was jammed full of the ugliest looking citizens you can imagine. I called the police and said, "You better get over here. It looks terrible to me." In the early morning hours Priscilla Ames's daughter Gwen was found murdered in the bushes near the Plaza. It was terrible. That may have been the time when the arch over the steps next to the Jasmine Café was the drug center for Reston. If you wanted drugs all you had to do was go to the arch.

Fonseca

The inclusion of beauty, art, and fantasy was important to us. We wanted to have some sculpture in our first village center.[45] I was put in touch with a fellow named Gonzalo Fonseca, a sculptor of some note

---

[44] Bob's stepdaughter.
[45] Lake Anne Village Center.

out of Manhattan. He came here and I was very businesslike with him. I told him we'd pay for three pieces; I forget what the amount was. What I hadn't known was that his wife was loaded, so money wasn't the object. He took an apartment in Herndon, spent 6 months here – he did the underpass, the sun boat downstairs, and the pylon. His charge was to design something the kids could climb on, to create humor we all could participate in.

"His charge was to design something the kids could climb on, to create humor we all could participate in."

Jane Wilhelm had fond memories of working with the artist.

"Fonseca loved it here. He made a post with an oval-shaped hole.[46] I asked him what it was. His English wasn't very good. He said, "You no know? I let you know." A few days later, he brought a child with him. The child walked up to the sculpture and immediately assumed the fetal position in the oval. I understood: it's to make the children feel safe. Like the boat in the cement,[47] he made that because he thought the mothers would be afraid for their children to play in the water but not in the boat. They all came out of this amazing man's head."

---

[46] The Pylon.
[47] The Sun Boat.

Community

The question was – what would we provide for people when they moved in. That was one of our big deals. We weren't going to let them wait five, ten, fifteen years – we'd give it to them when they moved in. So there were the athletic things that were obvious – playing fields, tennis, golf, swimming. I favored soccer and hoped baseball wouldn't catch on because I figured it was good for kids to have exercise and there's not any exercise worth mentioning in baseball. Baseball is largely a spectator sport for the players as well as the fans. We started off with a lot of soccer. We did a multipurpose court off North Shore Drive. It was soon known as "Simon's Folly" because no one used it. We had that asphalt court striped off for four different courts – volleyball, badminton, ring toss, and I don't remember the fourth one.

Jane Wilhelm recalled,

"Bob talked to me about the community facilities he'd like to include and those he'd like to exclude. He was very much opposed to competition; he thought cooperation was more important. He didn't want any Little Leagues here. I told him we'd have trouble keeping Little League out of here, they are the darlings."

Much later in life, while never changing his views on the merits of baseball, Bob came around enough to serve as the regular guest of honor for the Reston Little League's Opening Day Ceremonies. Many a player heard Bob's annual admonishment to remember, "The umpire is always right."

To fund community facilities, Bob set aside $190,000 for the initial expenses for the nonprofit Reston Virginia

Foundation for Community Programs, Inc. As its first executive director, Jane Wilhelm was tasked with assembling a board of 12 members to give advice to Bob and his staff.

Jane remembered,

"We had quite an interesting board. Bob wanted distinguished Virginians to make a better atmosphere in the community. We invited Leslie Cheek Jr., the founder and director of the Virginia Museum of Art in Richmond, and Dr. Douglas Southall Freeman, a Pulitzer Prize winner for biographies of Robert E. Lee and George Washington. Bob also wanted to identify people representing colleges and institutions. That was easy for me, I was on the board at Virginia Tech. Marshall Hahn, Tech's new president, was enthusiastic and had all sorts of ambitions. He was happy to join the Reston board.

Bob had many contacts himself in music, art, and literature. He got one of the most interesting, Michael Straight,[48] and Robert Porterfield, founder of the Barter Theater in Abingdon. Bob had an instinct that he needed a lot of Virginia support. He got Bob Porterfield on the board right away. Every one of the board members was just dedicated to this whole idea of the New Town. They were a tremendous help."

Horse Country

In the 1960s this was horse country. We fantasized that there would be horses here forever. We had Chuck Goodman, the distinguished architect who did Hickory Cluster, design a stable with an indoor riding ring. This was a place where people could park their horses when they wanted to and someone else would take care of feeding them and grooming them and everything. We had do-it-yourself stables scattered around the neighborhoods. The idea was that you rented a stall and you'd do everything. So we had the fantasy that Hunters Woods would be a place of bridle paths coming in and hitching posts.

---

[48] Editor and publisher of the *New Republic*, novelist, arts patron, and confessed KGB spy.

"We had do-it-yourself stables scattered around the neighborhoods." Artist's rendering.

Reston's Central Park

Our plan for Baron Cameron Park would bring tears to your eyes. Baron Cameron was to be Central Park. It was to have all the features of Central Park: ball fields, areas where people could walk and sit, and gardens and a perimeter of dense mid-rise residential. Once a year the steeplechase would take place. The folks with the apartments would invite their friends and

relatives to sit on the balcony to drink beer and watch the horses thunder under their balconies a la Siena.

Back then, Reston was in the heart of the Virginia hunt country. We hosted a well-attended, annual steeplechase off what is now Baron Cameron Avenue. Although it was illegal at the time in the Commonwealth, bets on the races could be placed at tote boards with State Police standing by for protection.

Child Care

I took a position that is not a very popular one. Child care is for parents. The goal was to get child care as good as what the kids would have at home. That was the minimal standard. To the extent that it was better, that was fine but it shouldn't add to the cost. I thought that child care should be available seven days a week, 24 hours a day. The main resource should be homes, the institutions should be training grounds, and that everybody who wanted to do it at home should be certified. The certification would not follow a set pattern, but would relate to the individual depending on their aptitude. It was important to us that the first people moving in had child care.

Along with the arts, child care was Bob's pet project. Jane Wilhelm asked him, "How does it happen that you're so fascinated with day care and nursery school?" He told her that whether they work outside the home or not, all women need someplace to put their kids once in a while. Tasked with finding a director for Reston's first child care facilities, Jane tapped a friend, Dorothy Bearman, to run Lake Anne Nursery Kindergarten (LANK).

Roof-top playground class at the Nursery-Kindergarten

While they awaited completion of their building, LANK started with five children in a model home in Hickory Cluster. Jane recalled,

"We all went for the Grand Opening. Bob was there right on time. One of the little boys, Michael Leary, the four-year-old son of one of the early builders, arrived by tricycle all the way from South Shore Road. He'd taken the pathways through Lake Anne. When Bob saw Mike riding his tricycle down the street he said, 'You know, that gives me real faith that the Reston Master Plan is going to work because you should be able to commute without needing an automobile.'"

LANK flourished under Dorothy's direction and Bob kept up on the school's progress. As Jane noted,

"We were so busy you could hardly get through the days. One staff member complained to me that Bob hadn't read his memo. He wanted me to intervene. Bob was not someone you interfered with. So I told this fellow, if you want to be sure he reads your memo, have Dorothy Bearman include it in the LANK Bulletin. Bob read that from beginning to end. He just adored LANK and Dorothy."

The coming Reston elementary school

"Reston just drew in enthusiastic, willing, excited people."

Schools

Bob hoped to get a few school buildings that didn't look like factories. To that end, Carol Lubin wrote a grant proposal and secured $15,000 from the Education Facilities Laboratory of the Ford Foundation for the architectural design of Lake Anne School.

Jane noted,

"That is why Lake Anne elementary school is the first and probably only school in Fairfax County that doesn't look like a factory. Its first principal was Beatrice Ward. She was excellent. Reston just drew in enthusiastic, willing, excited people. When you get people like that, you're going to be successful."

Churches

We asked the churches to come together to figure out how many church sites they would need for what we imagined would be a population of 80,000 people. The denominations came to a meeting in the Bowman House and proposed a total of 32 churches. And by a wild coincidence, in 1998 there are 32 congregations in Reston. I had a fantasy that in the Year 2000 there would be a book published of the churches of Reston. It would be a grand show of architecture.

I told them I felt it was a public relations stunt for developers to give sites to churches for free. If they wanted me to, I would, but I'd prefer to sell them the church sites at prevailing value so that we'd have more money to use for community facilities. That sounded good to them. I suggested we establish the price by invoking the Golden Rule. At that point they all paled. I offered to let each denomination proffer a price and there would be no negotiations. The first two transactions were done on that basis – one for the Methodists and the other for the Baptists.

Jane Wilhelm recollected, "Bob thought it would be a good idea to save space and also make it a more sociable and neighborly community if at least three denominations occupied the same site. They could decide among themselves how they wanted to build and use the space. The first purchaser of

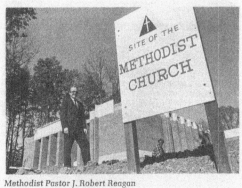

Methodist Pastor J. Robert Reagan

a plot of land was a Methodist church. It later became the United Christian Parish (UCP) – they were the only ones that really followed through on Bob's idea."

The type of interfaith cooperation Bob pioneered caught on in later years. The St. John Newman Catholic Church regularly allows its neighbor, the Northern Virginia Hebrew Congregation (NVHC), to use their space for larger events. Similarly, NVHC makes their facility available to a local Muslim congregation.

Cemeteries

The planners wanted to have a cemetery; they put it in the plan, but I nixed it. It was at the edge of Reston, near Lake Fairfax Park. But I was horrified by the whole funeral industry, especially the salesmanship of the casket industry. That was really quite sickening. I found the whole thing repulsive. I wasn't too sharp; I should have found a way to deal with it without feeling tainted by the business. It was a mistake I made. There are people who are still angry at me for this.

Now I like the idea of a virtual cemetery. Even better, buy a brick to commemorate the departed and raise money for the Reston Museum. My family has a plot. My mother got a huge stone, a boulder the size of a coffee table. Her ashes are in there and my first wife's. There's a plaque for each person. But no one ever goes there. I am sure none of the grandchildren even knows it exists. At any rate, the idea of going every five years and laying some flowers does not appeal to me. So this brick thing is a fine idea.

When my cousin Will died he was cremated. His ashes were put in a can. My mother gave them to me and instructed me to release them in Long Island Sound, where I was living at the time. Well, I put them in the attic and forgot about them. I sold the house. Years later the phone rang and the new owner said, "You son of a bitch, my son was up in the attic playing and got into the ashes. You come here and take them away!"

When I die, I'll give my body to the interns, let them use it. I'd be more than happy for someone to use my eyes, or liver, but if it's not useful, I'll be laboratory material. When my time comes I'm giving my body to science. Listen, I know they'll toss it around, have a food fight, and so forth. Of course! But what's the difference? You're dead. If Cheryl does a good job it will all be used. I think it is an awful waste not to use everything.

Gulf Reston

In 1964 I was looking for a godfather. Someone introduced me to Gulf and we went into a long series of negotiations. It was tense going because we were hawking our land. The first deal was, they'd invest $15 million in our project and they would get a preferred position and a small share of the equity. They would get all the gas stations that we would generate. They'd also have the opportunity to build oil distribution points so there would be central oil tanks. The Gulf executive went down to Florida to see if they could get their guys to cooperate. They came up with a deal. They agreed to $15 million but we had to pay off the $12 million interest fee with a ten-year mortgage.

I approached Smith Bowman and asked for a discount on the mortgage. He didn't want to discount it at all; it was a perfectly good mortgage. Smith Bowman tooled around the narrow Reston lanes in his Rolls-Royce with his handsome young bride. He was a Princeton-educated architect. He built a warehouse right past the pond on Sunset Hills Road. It had Greek columns that didn't quite reach the ground. I was up the creek and had to take Gulf's deal, and did. We paid off the mortgage with $10 million. That left us $4.2, which disappeared the day it arrived to all the loans we had. Gulf negotiated a loan with John Hancock Insurance Company for us. It would be $100 million today. That kept us going for quite some time.

"We had a fantastic array of attendees."

Reston Grand Openings

We had two grand openings. That made the first grand opening people sore I think. I have not got them separate in my head. We had a fantastic array of attendees: Stephen Spender, US Poet Laureate, who was to write a poem for the occasion; and Augie Heckscher.[49] We had ambassadors from several countries. Bob Weaver, Secretary of Housing was there, and the Secretary of the Interior, my tennis partner, Stewart Udall was there. We had three brass choirs, one on top of Heron House, one on top of the J Building, and one in the part of it where the fountain is now. Acoustics were considered in the design of the J Building. That was thrilling. We also commissioned a musical work. That was a big show and then we had another one.

[49] August Heckscher II served as President Kennedy's Special Consultant on the Arts and Parks Commissioner of New York City.

The first grand opening, held on Saturday, December 4, 1965, was billed as "A Salute to the Arts." Attended by 12,000 visitors and likely all 700 residents, the dedication of Lake Anne Plaza featured poetry, music, and dance. As Bob explained in the December 1965 Reston Times, "We are doing this because one of the concepts underlying the creation of Reston is that its residents should be provided with the opportunity for a good life. Moreover, the residents of Reston intend the arts to play a prominent role in community life."

The Dedication of Reston

The second grand opening served as the official dedication of Reston. Guest speakers at the May 21, 1966, Dedication Day included Virginia Governor Mills E. Godwin and Secretaries Udall and Weaver. Secretary Weaver awarded Bob HUD's first Urban Pioneer Award. Also in attendance were ambassadors from 22 countries and the guests of honor – the First Families of Reston. During this event, Secretary Udall, announced plans for the government to build a $50 million headquarters for the United States Geological Survey (USGS) complex in Reston. A telegram from President Johnson declared, "In this age of ever-mounting urban growth, the birth of a New Town such as Reston is a living influence which invigorates our concepts of urban planning. I extend greetings to all of you as you dedicate the City of Reston."

Jane Wilhelm reminisced about this beautiful spring day:
"Everyone was so happy. A planeload of planners and architects were flown down here to attend at Bob's expense. The poet in residence at the Library of Congress, Stephen Spender, stood up in the Lake Anne Plaza pulpit and read "Atticus." He said he intended to write his own poem, but couldn't come up with one that satisfied him. Anne Simon wrote and read a poem. She was very interested in the whole project. She put her heart and soul into this whole thing. We had so many dignitaries there, including cabinet members. I was a little bit acquainted with Stewart Udall, Secretary of the Interior. I had one of his children,

Scott Udall, in 8th grade English class. On the day I was teaching prefixes and suffixes, Scott Udall suddenly looked very thoughtful and raised his hand to offer an example. He said, "I know a good one, my father thinks that the problem with Kennedy's cabinet is that it's filled up with pseudo-intellectuals."

Reston Players

When there were 400 men, women, and children living here, a resident named Frank Matthews came in to see me in my office. He and a group of friends wanted to form a theatrical company. He asked for permission to use the riding center Charles Goodman had designed. That was amusing to me because we had planned to have a consultant come in to see if it was feasible to do a production there. Matthews was emphatic in telling me that all his group wanted was use of the ring – they were not interested in any advice or financial contribution. I agreed and they set forth.

They were intent on setting up a permanent organization and raising the astonishing amount of $5,000 ($25,000 in today's dollars) to use as a revolving fund. This was to be their nest egg. There was no mistake that one could imagine that they didn't make. Rather than play it safe with *Our Town* or equivalent for their first production they decided to do an original, a musical, set not in sunny Virginia but on Wall Street. Of the total population of 400 Restonians, almost 100 became involved in the production as writers, musicians, actors, stage crew, and publicists – all while also doing their day jobs.

During casting a young black lady tried out for a particular role but was rejected. They were so eager to have a black girl in the show to demonstrate how far Reston had come in integrating they asked her what she could do.

She said tap dancing, so they developed a part for her in the show. That lady was Beverly Cosham. She went on to a successful singing career. And the group went on to be the Reston Players. I love this story because it shows the feeling of community that existed early on.

Greater Washington Pro Tennis Tournament

Bob announced to his staff, "We've got to have a tennis tournament." That Reston didn't yet have a court worried him none. "We can build one, can't we?" Jane Wilhelm recalled,

"The project was completed just days before the players arrived. We had a clay court and bleachers. This was a tremendous public relations event. Bob brought in the world's best players to put on a demonstration and offer coaching. Sargent Shriver came – there were more Kennedys here than anyone else."

Bob managed to lure the prestigious Greater Washington International Professional tournament, traditionally held in Rock Creek Park in DC, to his freshly created courts. The event brought more than 1,500 spectators to the new facility and more importantly, to his fledgling New Town. Those who came were treated to spirited matches between some of the world's greatest players including Pancho Gonzales (ranked 1st in the world, 1952–1960), Ken Rosewall (ranked 1st, 1962–1963), Andres Gimeno (ranked 6th, 1960), Pancho Segura (ranked 1st, 1952), Butch Buchholz (1960 US Open and Wimbledon Champion), and Rod Laver.

GREATER WASHINGTON INTERNATIONAL PROFESSIONAL

TENNIS

TOURNAMENT
June 23 through June 27

Reston, Virginia

A member of the grounds crew, John S. Withers Jr., noted,

"The players were friendly to both the staff and fans who would come to the courts in early afternoon before competition began around 4:00 p.m. Tennis balls, racquets, and hats were signed and distributed and the players would sit on patio furniture set up around the court and talk to the fans. On Saturday afternoon, June 27, Rosewall defeated Laver in two sets, capturing the 1965 Greater Washington Pro Tennis Tournament, the first major sports event to be held in Reston."

The excitement and momentum generated by the event continued to fuel tournaments, albeit with less high-profile players.

Ford Foundation

As financial pressures mounted, exacerbated by the 1966 housing recession, Bob explored additional funding sources. Jane Wilhelm recollected,

"Bob said we might as well try to write some grant proposals to the Ford Foundation as Bob had some contacts there. The Ford Foundation Director, Mc-George Bundy, came down and we toured him through the entire place which was largely still under construction. At the end of the day, we gathered together and adjourned to the Quay Club. It was a wonderful place. To this day, I can see Bob sitting up very straight in a chair with Bundy arranged on the couch with all the Reston brochures laid out in front of him. And Bundy is telling Bob this sad story of why the Ford Foundation couldn't fund it. It was just a sad thing. But Bob persevered. Reston never would have materialized if Bob hadn't been so stubborn. It really wouldn't. He would undertake to do something that every single person on his staff thought was crazy and it would succeed."

Quay Club

Prohibition, as it related to serving alcoholic beverages in restaurants, was still the law of the land in Virginia in the late 1960s. Reston's only establishment with liquor rights was a private bottle club known as the Quay Club. For three dollars you got a liquor locker, a membership card, and a place to have a drink on the Plaza.

Jane Wilhelm clearly loved the place, but she remembered that not everyone was so pleased.

"There was a person who was very critical of one thing we had done. He complained to Bob that he thought that it was a very serious matter that we had located a church right in the sight line of a liquor club; it was immoral, depraved, and would ruin the youth of the community. I didn't know what Bob was going to say. Bob didn't hesitate. He said, 'Now sir, it's getting to be a complicated world. Kids don't always understand adults. But when the little children in Reston grow up they'll see that everybody goes to church but only adults go to the liquor clubs.' "

World Renown

Planners, politicians, and New Town enthusiasts came from around the world to see Bob's creation. Jane Wilhelm noted their passion for the project.

"Amongst the people who came were world-famous, elderly, city planners. It was almost as if they had a personal stake in the completion and success in this planned community – as if they had had the same dream that never came to fruition."

Jane remarked that one visitor in particular caused quite a stir.

"Early in the morning on July 25, 1967, I got an urgent phone call from our public relations man, Bernie Norwitch. He said, 'Get to the office in a hurry. Lady Bird Johnson is visiting Reston at noon today.' When I arrived thirty minutes later everyone was manicuring the place. I remember getting down on my hands and knees and weeding the Plaza."

"It was particularly exciting shepherding Lady Bird Johnson along the village pathways."

It was particularly exciting shepherding Lady Bird Johnson along the village pathways. For security reasons, we had little advance notice of her arrival so there was no way to alert the community of her visit. However, she and I had not gone very far before the grapevine heralded her approach and our pathways became lined by enthusiastic citizens.

Mrs. Johnson was a gracious, well-informed visitor, and the children followed her around like the Pied Piper. As we approached Fonseca's boat sculpture there was a lot of excited screaming. I asked the children, What is all the ruckus? They pointed excitedly and exclaimed, sharks!

The Nudist Colony and the Bunny Man

Growing up in Reston, there were two prevailing urban legends: our origins as a nudist colony and the terrifying tale of the "Bunny Man." During our interviews, Jane Wilhelm shed light on the first, which shined a little light on the second.

"One day Carol Lubin said to me, 'Did you ever hear of Snake Den Lake? Let's go down there.' She said someone told her it was a nudist colony. We took out the company jeep. We got mired in the mud on 60-Foot Road[50] – it wasn't yet paved.

We finally found the site with a map and a compass. It was totally surrounded by an overgrown thorny Mayberry bush used as a hedge. And inside the hedge was a rusty barbed-wire fence. I said, What are we going to do now? Carol was much more adventurous than I'd ever imagined. She said, 'Well, we'll just have to climb this fence.' I could not fathom climbing that fence. But she thought ahead. She had brought along some heavy clippers. We managed to clip a break in the barbed wire fence. Then we gradually got through the hedge to get in there. Well, it was an absolutely crazy thing to do. We were so scratched up and bleeding. It was really a deserted place. Bob and his planners must have been down here when they were buying the land but I don't think they ever came in.

50 An early incarnation of Reston Avenue.

We saw a few old shelters boarded up for the summer. So we concluded that it had indeed been a nudist colony. Bob didn't want to talk about it.

I really wondered about the nudist colony through the years; I never heard anything. Then one day a man came into the pharmacy. He seemed to be looking for something. I finally said,

Is there anything I can help you with? He hesitated and said, 'Well, there really is. When I was a child, my parents brought me here. We spent our summers here on a lake.' I couldn't hide the smile on my face. I said, Well, people around here say it was a nudist colony. He looked quite relieved and confirmed the story. Then he lamented, 'I'd just really like to see it again.'"

The Forest Green Nudist Colony disbanded in 1949 after member Charles Holober was convicted of killing his wife and child. His 1968 release from the Southwestern State mental hospital roughly coincided with the first Bunny Man sightings and fueled an urban legend of a costumed boogeyman. Several localities claim the Bunny Man as their own and each adds a sprinkle of local flavor. The common thread is an agitated, possibly murderous, axe- (sometimes hatchet)

Artist's rendering of the mythic character.

wielding man dressed in a bunny suit. Whether he is an escaped convict or a furry protestor of encroaching residential development, for decades local teens[51] have recounted surviving late night excursions to the Bunny Man Bridge (Fairfax Station) or the Bunny Man House (Reston). Since the first sightings in the early 1970s, the legend has inspired a sub-genre of Bunny Man-inspired artwork, literature, and even a rock musical by the band Mantua Finials.

---

[51] Many stories include the Bunny Man skulking after meddling teens on Halloween.

Beginning of the End

Gulf Oil sent Bob Ryan from Cabot, Cabot & Forbes[52] down here as a consultant to tell them if they should continue funding our operation. When he said he "would like to see us hang by our fingernails," I knew we were in serious trouble. Ryan decided on his first visit here that he wanted my job. I could tell immediately that I was in trouble with him. He was passionately wooing everyone in the organization while sneering at me. It was perfectly evident that he wanted me out.

R H. RYAN
... takes over at Reston

Gulf Corp. Takes Over At Reston

General Electric

I read in a publication that the president of General Electric was looking to build 20 New Towns, starting one every nine months. They had a group of 60 people working on developing the database for this effort. I decided that was where I should be rather than taking a shellacking from Bob Ryan. So I went to Louisville, Kentucky, where GE had the people I wanted to talk to initially. I worked with them and they got very excited. It was obvious that if they were going to do these 20 New Towns it would be a great timesaver for them to buy Reston and use it as their laboratory for the rest of their efforts. The logic was unassailable.

As time went on, they decided to send a bunch of people up here to go through our books. I remember telling our staff, they should show them everything except our conclusions because it would be invaluable to us to learn how to organize our material. Clearly these people were more sophisticated than we were. They would know how to do it. If it didn't go through, at

---

[52] A real estate consulting firm.

least we'd learn how to organize our material. To my utter amazement, these people decided to use our figures. They presented it up the line in GE until finally they got to the top guy before the final board. This was the executive vice president in charge of appropriating $50 million of development funds. When he approved it the GE guys on this team brought their wives to Reston and got involved in picking their houses. We reserved office space for them: it was a done deal. The deal would have been sensational for my family and for me. We would have made a substantial profit, retained 20% of the equity, been relieved of all debt, and I would have been a key figure in building 20 New Towns.

I went up to New York to sit with the chairman of the board who had his office on one of the top floors of the GE building on Lexington Avenue. I've been in a few places like this, NBC, CBS, etc. They all have one thing in common. It appears that nothing is going on. William Paley at CBS has an anteroom filled with antiques where you waited before going to see him. This GE person didn't have all that culture; he just had a big room, two secretaries – they had the whole floor to themselves. We had a very fine talk. I thought it was all set. Then it went "to the executive" as they call it. They operated like the Gulf people did. They did everything unanimously. One board member could not agree to GE's becoming involved in an integrated community. And his fellow board members could not imagine GE building anything but 20 lily-white communities. As a result, GE abandoned its New Town program. That was the kiss of death for their whole project. It was the kiss of death for me too because at that point, we were hanging out to dry.

In Cold Blood

When GE said no, I had to call Gulf and tell them that I couldn't go any further. There was a meeting in New York and in front of each of us was a portfolio. I told my friend Bill Henry, who had hoped to be chairman, that they picked him to be the gopher to fire us. He was a 240-pound, ex-football player and a hell of a good guy. I implored him, "Whatever you do, don't turn this thing over to Bob Ryan." When I opened up my portfolio, Ryan was listed as president and I was chairman of the board. Ryan had recommended that they take all of my family's assets, because I had signed promissory notes. Ryan's recommendation was that they wipe us out.

Bill Henry laid out the relationship with Gulf: they could take everything we had. I said to him, "Certainly you didn't come here to tell me that, there must be something else you have in mind." Turns out he did, he was going to release us from all of our debts and give us a special class of stock for our investment of $2 million bucks. So I knew when I sat down that we weren't going to be wiped out but I didn't know it meant Bob Ryan would be president.

Soon after there was a board meeting in Reston. The Gulf boys from Pittsburgh and Bob Ryan were there. As chairman of the board I was running the meeting. Ryan characterized my contribution as developer as "financial mismanagement" and used this occasion to make fun of everything we had done. He gave a slide show designed to embarrass us. One of the first slides he showed was the Esso[53] sign juxtaposed with the directional sign to Reston. Then he ridiculed Reston's seven goals. He said, "Look where he puts making money – at the bottom of the list." Everyone laughed.

[53] Gulf's competitor.

Jane Wilhelm was also at the meeting and recalled Bob Ryan's demeanor. "He announced, 'We're going to make several changes in the way this place is run.' He went down the line of Bob's staff and pointed them out one by one. He said, 'You will go, you will stay.' It went on down like that. It was terrible. It was so crass. And Bob (Simon) is never crass."

When the meeting was over, Bill Henry said, "You're going to have to resign." I said no, "I'm not going to resign; they'll have to fire me." So he said, "Okay, you are fired." That's how it went.

And so, as *New York Times* architecture critic Ada Louise Huxtable put it, "Overnight Reston went from one man's dream to a corporate subsidiary."

Jane added, "Anne Simon was so distraught when Bob was forced to leave. Gulf gave them 24 hours to vacate the Bowman House. That famous day they left, Anne left a copy of <u>In Cold Blood</u> in the center of the bed where the new head of Reston, Bob Ryan was going to sleep. He deserved it."

Simon Says Good-Bye

An open letter:

I am thankful for this opportunity to communicate with you, the citizens of Reston. I profoundly regret that my connection with the future development of Reston has been severed. I shall treasure the associations that I have had with you in the past several years.

Reston has made a fine start. Working together, we have learned much about what makes a good community. Key ingredients are respect for all individuals, opportunities for participation in recreational and cultural activities, and good design. Reston has proved its economic feasibility; what it lacked was capital. This is now to be supplied.

I trust that you as individuals and through your many existing organizations, as well as those to come, will work constructively with Gulf Reston Inc.

Collectively you have a signal opportunity to further explore human and community relations. It is my hope that in so doing, you will discover ways to make your lives richer which will, in turn, serve as inspiration for the improvement of many other communities of men.

Robert E. Simon, Jr.

Farewell, Reston

There followed an emotional farewell on the Plaza with community members.

Early Reston executive James Selonick reflected on that event:

"What I remember most vividly was the day that Bob left Reston when the whole community turned out to render praise and cheer. The newspaper said it was the first time in history that a developer had been honored by the people who lived in the project the developer had created. I am still cheering."

Bob was tight-lipped and close to tears as he told the crowd, "It would be a mistake not to assume the best. I do. And you all are entitled to it." Lynn Lilienhal noted, "When Reston failed, it was like someone dying. It was devastating to Bob, to our family, to the community."

Part 4: Exile and Homecoming

I was persona non grata. I had to leave.

Bob returned to New York, got divorced, remarried, and accepted consulting jobs and speaking engagements. Bob shared little with me about this time. When pressed, he'd recount a few resume highlights: conducting fact-finding tours on Indian reservations for Secretary Udall, attempting to impose order upon a chaotic Tegucigalpa Street grid, and reviewing a land reclamation project in the Philippines for President Ferdinand Marcos. (The Marcos job afforded him a ringside seat to the historic heavyweight championship fight between Muhammad Ali and Joe Frazier known as the "Thrilla in Manila.") But Bob showed none of the obvious delight in reliving these memories as he did with earlier ones. It is no surprise then, to hear family members describe Bob during this time as lonely, depressed, and longing for the community he sought to create in Reston.

Returning to Reston

Over the years, I'd returned to Reston occasionally, at least once a year, especially at festival time. They'd wave me around like a flag. So as my business was winding down in the early '90s I started to consider coming back to Reston. I was living on Long Island with 4,500 square feet of housing for a family on 10 acres of grounds and woods. And it turned out that the family didn't come out here. I was more or less isolated. A hermit gets his kicks out of solitude. I am anti-hermit. I get my kicks out of people. Children, relatives, neighbors – that's where you get happiness. It appealed to me to join the Reston community, so that's what I did.

In the documentary *Another Way of Living*, Bob's widow Cheryl Terio-Simon added, "Bob had been living on Long Island and it had been very lonely for him. He had other properties and other consulting gigs but nothing inspired the passion in him that Reston had inspired. This is his magnum opus."

I called Julia Keane and asked her to see what she could find. She found 1503 Heron House, Lake Anne, Reston, Virginia. I got ready to move and had a fire sale. I asked Julia to measure the elevator to see if we could get the piano up. The dimensions were fine, the piano would fit. After I got here, for at least a year, people would ask me, "How did you get the piano in here?"

Jane Wilhelm was among a small group aware of Bob's return.

"When he decided to move down here he admonished me not to tell anyone he was coming. I didn't tell a soul. I was apprehensive about him coming. You know what they say about native New Yorkers – they can never live anywhere else. And he never did live anywhere else. When he was building Reston he still lived in New York. He spent Monday–Friday here but went home to New York on the weekends. After he left he'd come down and stay with Lynn,[54] so people still thought he was around. But he came back for good in 1993 and it was just amazing. Not long after he met Cheryl. Of course that's why he looks so happy here. But even before that, he never showed an inkling that he shouldn't have left New York. Two years after he got here he told me one night looking out at Lake Anne, "I'm happier than I've ever been in my whole life!" And I said, "Why shouldn't you be? This is your town."

It was a great time to come back, all the hoopla. Front page stories in the papers. It was great to see everybody. I wasn't a hermit anymore, I was in a community.

---

[54] His stepdaughter Lynn Lilienthal.

Cheryl noted, "When he returned here there might have been a question in
is mind about how he'd be received." The next twenty years would demonstrate
e had nothing to worry about.

Meeting Cheryl

On July 18, I got in the elevator on the 15th floor to take a walk. When the
elevator stopped on the 13th floor, a young lady entered. She had walking
shoes on and I asked her if she'd like to join me for a walk. That of course
was Cheryl. And the rest is history.

Bob and Cheryl travelled the world together. They strolled the streets of
'aris; trekked through Machu Picchu; walked along the Great Wall of China,
ruised the Baltic, the Rhône, the Danube, and the Nile; rode camels in Petra;
oared in a hot air balloon over the
unes of Namibia; rode dog sleds in the
Canadian Rockies; and were carried atop
palanquins in Ajanta, India.

Bob and Cheryl in Egypt.   *Bob and Cheryl in Jordan.*

Bob and Cheryl seated in Box 23 at Carnegie Hall.

But one of her fondest memories involves a local date that for anyone other than Bob would have been a series of unfortunate events.

Eager to evaluate the hype over the Inn at Little Washington for himself, and hoping to impress his new love, Bob planned a weekend getaway. Things did not start well.

After mistakenly putting regular gas into his diesel Mercedes, the car sputtered and died on busy Interstate 66. These were the days before the convenience of cell phones allowed a rescue call to a friend or AAA. But somehow they encountered a flatbed tow truck that carried the car, Bob, and Cheryl to a nearby service station.

When Bob realized he'd left something in the car, he climbed up on the flatbed to retrieve it. Cheryl watched in horror as Bob lost his footing and began to fall headfirst from the elevated lift. But, as noted in his baby book some 80 years earlier, Bob demonstrated impressive athleticism. Perhaps calling on muscle memory from his diving days, Bob turned the free fall into a somersault and nailed the landing.

With that catastrophe averted, the next hurdle was getting to the Inn at Little Washington. Unbidden, the service station owner offered up his own car for the weekend so they could resume their special date. Cheryl summed up the outing this way, "That's just the way things happened when you were with Bob. More often than not he came up smelling like roses."

Reston Association Board

Despite his plans to focus on gardening and other leisure pursuits, Bob quickly added his voice to debates over local hot-button issues of the day. When the Reston Land Corporation gave up its seat on the Reston Association Board, Bob submitted his statement of candidacy.

When I came back to Reston. I had lots of ideas for stimulating nature development. I got the feeling that I wasn't getting anyplace at all because I didn't have any credentials; I was a private citizen. I thought what the hell, I'll run for the Reston Association board and that'll be very different. This was 1996. It was a fine campaign. I won by the biggest margin ever.[55]

But it's so slow; the bureaucratic process is so slow. It's one thing to be a CEO and you've got a problem and if you've got any brains at all you consult with people, get a wide range of viewpoints, and then finally you decide what to do and that's the end of it. The democratic process is quite different.

85th Birthday

Bob began the night before his 85th birthday much as he did his original one - enclosed in a warm, dark space, waiting to be delivered but content to stay put until the moment was right. It was the second Friday of the month and Bob had

---

[55] Bob captured 70% of the votes cast.

just enjoyed an evening of dinner, several martinis, and intellectual inquiry with the Philosophers.[56] Heading for home, Bob stepped into the elevator, pushed 13, floated a bit and then stopped well short of his destination.

> **I was in there** a few hours. I banged on the wall a little bit but that didn't do any good. A darling lady who lived on the second floor came over and talked to me. She gathered other people and Cheryl. Meanwhile I was lying down on the floor trying to go to sleep but every so often people banged on the door asking how I was doing and woke me up! The elevator repairman freed me sometime around 2:00 a.m.

Untold Stories (aka Bronze Bob)

In early 2004, the Reston Historic Trust began planning a celebration for Bob's birthday. Inspired by University of Virginia's annual Founder's Day celebration in honor of Thomas Jefferson's birthday, board member Chuck Veatch wanted to do something extraordinary. He thought Bob's 90th would be the perfect opportunity to start a similar tradition in Reston. Chuck wanted to honor Bob while giving the community an enduring gift. As Chuck explained, "My first thought was to put Bob on a horse at the intersection of Reston Parkway and Sunset Hills. Well, I knew we weren't going to pull that off." His second, more practical thought was a sculpture of Bob in Lake Anne. Chuck's vision was of "Something inviting, something that says, 'Come talk to me.' Let's put him on a bench, a smile on his face, put his arm up, inviting you to sit down a while."

Chuck commissioned sculptor and Reston native Zachary (Zack) Oxman to create the piece and secured financing through the generosity of the "Founder's Day Founders."

---

[56] According to Bob, an impressive group of interesting people who meet monthly for dinner and good conversation.

Throughout the process, Chuck knew keeping Bob in the dark would be difficult. If something was happening in Reston, especially something that required two architectural review board approvals, Bob knew about it.

Chuck enlisted Cheryl in a secret mission to take photos Zack could work from. Under the guise of trying out a new camera, Cheryl posed Bob on the bench exactly the way Chuck wanted him to appear in the sculpture. Zack worked up a clay model of Bob, but at a point in the process he needed the actual bench to ensure the measurements were exact. As Chuck explains,

"I called up the Reston Association to inform them we'd be stealing *the* bench. On a quiet weekday morning Zack drove in his van onto the Plaza. We quickly unbolted the bench. The bench was so heavy I recruited a bystander to help us. He was amused but satisfied with our explanation for taking it (part of an art project) and helped us heave it into the back of the van. Just as we get it in the van, here comes Bob. I said to the guy, you've got to leave now. Just walk away! Zack and I dove into the back of the van, shut the doors, and hid on the floor. Just as Bob was about to approach the van, an admirer started chatting with him. The conversation ended and thankfully Bob walked on to the bank. I slipped out the back and Zack sped out of the Plaza. Bob was none the wiser."

The night before the Founder's Day celebration, Zack, Chuck, and Phil Lilienthal[57] installed the sculpture *Untold Stories* (know as *Bronze Bob* to the rest of us). They covered it with a large tarp and paid a young man to guard it all night. Nobody knew what it was. As the climax of the celebration, the three men unveiled the sculpture. Bob was floored: he absolutely loved it.

[7] Husband of Bob's stepdaughter Lynn Lilienthal.

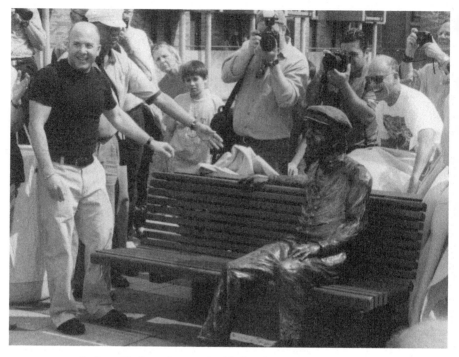

Sculptor Zachary Oxman (in black t-shirt) and Phil Lilienthal (wearing sunglasses and holding white drape) reveal Untold Stories.

More than once during my daily walk around Lake Anne, kids from the day care will look at me, and then the statue, and then back at me. One day, a little boy asked me, "How'd you get out?"

A Century and a Half

In 2014 the community gathered to celebrate Bob's 100th birthday and Reston's 50th. Chuck Veatch kicked things off with a reading from Bob's prophetic dedication of Reston 50 years earlier. "It is a place where people will come to live, work, play and call their own. From this day forward, Reston is its people."

Nearly 2,000 past and present Restonians, along with local politicians including Supervisor Cathy Hudgins, Delegates Ken Plum and Janet Howell, Congressman Gerry Connolly, Senator Tim Kaine, and Virginia Governor Terry McAuliffe packed the Plaza to celebrate.

Lynn Lilienthal and her grandchildren surprised Bob with a congratulatory letter from President Obama. He wrote,

"You are part of a generation that helped guide our country through uncertain and extraordinary times, and the energy and creativity you have shown over the years serve as an inspiration. As you celebrate a century of memories, I hope you take tremendous pride in the community you founded 50 years ago and all you have done to ensure our neighborhoods are vibrant places to live and work."

Ferried by pedicab, Bob arrived at the Reston Museum to cut his birthday cake and was literally mobbed by the crowd. Inside the museum he held court, talking to old friends and admirers one at a time while a line of well-wishers snaked out the door. He stayed for hours, loving it all. Cheryl recalled, "He was in his element, being acclaimed for his vision of the community he founded fifty years ago and for having reached 100 years as a healthy and exceedingly vivacious member of the community." Chuck Veatch added, "the celebration really highlighted how much he had become the symbol of all that was great about Community in Reston."

Saying Goodbye

In his later years, Bob liked to point out that (by choice) he was living in the smallest square footage he'd ever occupied, with the fewest possessions, and he had never been happier. Though it seemed impossible that terrible day he left Reston in 1967, Bob got a second chance to enjoy the community he created. He died there on September 21, 2015, after a brief illness. Despite his age, 101, the news of his passing stunned the community. Many had seen him weeks before gliding his "Cadillac-of-walkers" around the lake offering a robust, "Healthy, how 'bout you?" in response to queries about his well-being.

As the truth sank in, *Bronze Bob* became the focal point for tributes. Mourners left flowers, candles, notes, pictures, and bottles of Akvavit. Some shared his bench and toasted a final martini in his honor.

Several hundred mourners attended a grassroots vigil on the Plaza to find comfort in shared grief, to celebrate his life, and to express gratitude for their hometown and the community he inspired.

Bronze Bob *became the focal point for tributes.*

I am so pleased that you are having this community vigil tonight. It is the kind of remembrance that would be most meaningful to Bob.

Bob loved Lake Anne. He loved greeting and being greeted by Restonians and visitors alike. It was a great pleasure for him to sit on our balcony and watch the happenings on the plaza....probably with a martini... and appreciate anew the many wonderful details of what he called its "Modern Gothic Architecture."

Bob truly believed his oft-quoted assertion that community is what it is all about... and what a beautiful example is this wonderful gathering tonight to remember him.

Thank You All for this and the many, many expressions of love and respect for Bob.

-Cheryl Terio-Simon

Photo Credits:

Photos and other images courtesy of the personal collection of Robert E. Simon Jr. on pages: 2-12, 15, 16, 21-24, 26-31, 34, 36, 37, 48, 50, 53, 55, 63, 70, 71, 119

Photos and other images courtesy of the Carnegie Hall Archives on pages: 19, 20, 41, 45, 46, 47, 59

Photos and other images courtesy of the Reston Historic Trust on pages: 64, 66, 73, 74, 75 -77, 80, 82, 86-90, 92, 95, 97, 98, 99, 102, 104 -108, 111, 113, 114, 115, 116, 123, 124, 125 (lower half of page), 128

Letters courtesy of Carolyn Boyle on page 81

Photo courtesy of Ciao Fonseca on page 91

Photos courtesy of Kristina S. Alcorn on pages 93, 131

Image of Quay Club card courtesy Tom Langman on page 107

Original artwork courtesy of Eric MacDicken on page 110

Photo courtesy of Rebekah Wingert-Jabi on page 120

Photo (upper half of page) courtesy of Reston Now on page 125

Photo courtesy of the Reston Community Center ©Jim Kirby on page 126

Photo courtesy of Charlotte Geary on page 127

About The Author

Kristina S. Alcorn is a lifelong
Restonian, writer, photographer, and
lover of a well-told story. She lives
in Reston with her husband and
children and a revolving cast of feline
houseguests. This is her first book.

CPSIA information can be obtained
at www.ICGtesting.com
Printed in the USA
LVOW06*0815290416

485717LV00001BA/1/P